MW00657640

The importance of seeking qualified professional assistance for legal and financial concerns is emphasized throughout this book. Because everyone's situation is unique, material in this book cannot be treated as personal financial or legal advice. Such advice may only be provided as part of a thorough examination of an individual's specific circumstances.

Personal photographs published on the cover and throughout this book were donated by clients, family members and friends of the author. Subjects featured in these photographs are identified by their actual first names. However, names used in case studies in this book were changed to protect client confidentiality.

PRAISE FOR:
SAVING MOM AND DAD . . . AND YOU

"Robert Cullen has done a great job tackling one of the biggest mysteries in financial planning today. Planning for large medical expenses is now second only to 'Will I outlive my money?' among my clients' concerns. Robert's *Put it in a Box*™ concept is powerful and simple enough for anyone to understand. *Saving Mom and Dad…and You* also provides sage advice about handling relationships with family members and eligibility workers. Professional articles seldom handle the human aspect of this planning and this book provides useful tools for consumers and professionals alike. I will be recommending *Saving Mom and Dad…and You* to my clients because I believe it will be a great investment in their financial education."

— CHRISTIAN F. LI, CFP®; DIAMOND BAR, CA

"Robert Cullen has created a well-crafted explanation of the complex bureaucracy of Medi-Cal. These real-life scenarios are easily adapted to one's own personal situation. And sprinkled throughout this very readable book are numerous practical suggestions for dealing with aging–be it yours or your parents'."

— LINDA MAXWELL, PRIVATE CONSERVATOR; UPLAND, CA

"Great book–easy to read and understand. *Saving Mom and Dad…and You* gives the answers and solutions to questions I didn't even know how to ask! I plan to give a copy to my in-laws."

— JUDITH HARPER, CERTIFIED APPRAISER; COVINA, CA

"Takes a complex subject and translates it well for family members. The book uses excellent tables and graphs and shows great knowledge about the Medi-Cal process. It is written in an easy-to-understand style. It uses very good examples to explain a complicated process. This book explains a lot about the Medi-Cal process and clarifies how one can receive this much needed benefit."

— SANDY KNOX, BSN, PHN
VISITING NURSE ASSOCIATION OF SOUTHERN CALIFORNIA

"I had the opportunity to read your book and loved it. This is a book I would be happy to give my clients, as I believe it would assist them in understanding Medi-Cal and long-term care. This is a wonderful book!"

— CHRISTINA STONE, ATTORNEY, CERTIFIED SPECIALIST
ESTATE PLANNING, TRUST AND PROBATE LAW,
FAZIO & STONE; LA HABRA, CA

"Robert Cullen is a pro in this area. His book simplifies and makes the complex area of Medi-Cal and long-term care understandable both to consumers and to lawyers who need to know how to advise them. The book is on the shelf next to my desk for frequent and easy reference."

— JOHN P. HOWLAND, LL.B., ESTATE PLANNING ATTORNEY
BUXBAUM AND CHAKMAK; CLAREMONT, CA

SAVING MOM AND DAD . . . AND YOU

Senior Prom, 1945

SAVING MOM AND DAD . . . AND YOU

PLANNING FOR AND GETTING THROUGH THE MEDI-CAL AND LONG-TERM HEALTH CARE MINEFIELD – FOR CALIFORNIA BOOMERS AND THEIR AGING PARENTS

ROBERT J. CULLEN, CFP®

KP

Kelty Press
Upland, CA

SAVING MOM AND DAD . . . AND YOU

Copyright © 2004 by Robert J. Cullen, CFP®

All rights reserved. No part of this book may be reproduced or transmitted in any form or by any means, electronic or mechanical, including photocopying, recording, or by any information storage and retrieval system, without permission in writing from the publisher, except for brief quotations used in critical reviews and certain other non-commercial uses permitted by copyright law.

For permission requests, contact:

Kelty Press
818 N. Mountain Ave., Suite 102
Upland, CA 91786
909.985.4466
909.920.5460 Fax

www.keltypress.com
info@keltypress.com

Printed in the United States of America

ISBN 0-9749557-4-4
Library of Congress Control Number: 2004104963

Publisher's Cataloging-in-Publication Data available upon request

Book consultant: Ellen Reid
Cover artwork: Getty Images
Book cover and text design: Dotti Albertine

PHOTO CREDITS:
David, page 5, Studio 1921
Michael, page 5, Michael Taylor
Missouri stone barn and Nichols' round barn, page 116, Robert J. Cullen
Dave's cat, page 120, Robert J. Cullen

To Florence, my mother, for teaching me compassion
To Rose, my oldest sister, for her lifelong affection
To Elizabeth, my wife, for her constant love and support

FRED AND FRANCES, TWINS 1907

CONTENTS

PROLOGUE

HER RACE IS IRRELEVANT. Her image is universal: A refugee of life's wars. Her hair was brushed but not washed that morning. Her brownish pants and loose shirt were clean but faded and worn. She walked into the waiting room of the State Hearing office in a high-rise in downtown Los Angeles, her expression a mixture of wariness, fatigue and resolve. She was a middle-aged woman with a little spread about her waist who had come to fight The System. Unescorted by any professional counsel, she carried her papers in a loose stack, not in a folder or any visibly organized fashion.

Los Angeles is a large county containing amazing diversity. Rich to very poor. Sophisticated to very elementary. Cosmopolitan to rural. Her hands were calloused. Her arms and legs spoke of endurance and physical fortitude. She could be a farm woman. Or an artist. A sculptor, perhaps.

I had arrived forty-five minutes early for a Medi-Cal hearing to expand a client's Community Spouse Resource Allowance. As I explain in later chapters of this book, the outcome of these hearings is usually pre-ordained. The judge will approve the increase if the numbers are calculated correctly. Such hearings typically take 10 to 15 minutes and are heard at the state hearing level because county Medi-Cal personnel lack authority to grant such increases. I was waiting for my case to be called when the friendly young male receptionist called the middle-aged woman to the reception window.

"Ma'am," he began respectfully, "I looked up your case on the computer and it shows you postponed today's Medi-Cal hearing."

The woman was immediately exasperated. "I postponed the county hearing, not this one! I had two hearings scheduled for the same day at the same time. This is the more important one so I kept this one. Now you tell me it's been postponed?!"

After several exchanges, the young man excused himself and retreated into the unseen back office area. An older woman, probably his supervisor, came to the window. Though the supervisor spoke quietly, the middle-aged woman's voice grew louder with each exchange. Everyone in the waiting room looked nervously towards her. Was Security going to be called? The supervisor excused herself and the woman turned away from the window in disgust and sat angrily in the seat beside me.

She directed increasingly hostile comments towards the reception area where the young man was processing the next person's papers. Angry remarks about Medi-Cal's irresponsible bureaucracy and incompetent personnel escalated to pointed charges of rampant drug and alcohol use among all government workers. The woman lashed out like a proverbial wounded animal, angry and frustrated.

I was wondering how the situation would be resolved when a distinguished, well-dressed middle-aged man came through the office door into the reception area. His carriage and facial expression bespoke of judicial authority.

He approached the woman. "I am Judge ________," he began calmly: "I am an administrative law judge with the State. I would be the hearing officer for your Medi-Cal appeal if we had your case files." He stood while she sat. He spoke firmly without condescension. "But we don't have anything for your case because the County did not send anything over. I understand the County scheduled a hearing at the same time as this one. It appears that your beef is with them, not with us. We represent the State, not the County."

The woman shook her head, looking away from the judge. "It is not easy for me to get here," she said resignedly.

"I am very sorry for your trouble," the judge replied, his voice the proper mixture of empathy and professional restraint. He stepped back. The woman picked up the papers on her lap and stood. Shoulders slumped, she left quietly. She presented a broad, stoic back; the kind one sees in wartime photos of refugees walking resolutely through bombed ruins, their few possessions in their arms or piled high in a cart.

My case was called shortly thereafter. As expected, my hearing lasted less than 15 minutes. Without directly saying so, the judge indicated her decision would be in my client's favor.

Unlike the refugee, I left the building a victor. I stepped into the coffee shop wedged into the corner of the high-rise and rewarded myself with an iced coffee drink and calorie-laden crumb cake. I felt good. I had done my job. I retrieved my car from the underground garage and drove back to my office listening to pleasant music.

Yet I was troubled. The departing view of the frustrated woman stuck with me. She had not appeared mentally deficient or otherwise handicapped. Yet she was being ground down by rules and regulations that often prove incomprehensible to the people who most need to understand them.

During the preceding two years I had toyed with the idea of writing a book that would simplify Medi-Cal for consumers and their advisors. Within a week of that hearing, I resigned from two volunteer activities and began writing in earnest.

For supplying the motivation to get me started and committed to this project, I express my deepest gratitude to the unknown stoic refugee.

ROBERT J. CULLEN
SUMMER/FALL 2003

ABOUT THE AUTHOR

ROBERT J. CULLEN, CFP® is a writer, speaker and consultant with a gift for making complex issues understandable. He is the president of Cullen Financial Services, Inc., a full-range financial planning firm with special focus on the needs of elderly clients and their families. His work, coupled with experience as a reporter and financial journalist, propelled him to become an expert on the Medi-Cal system and the financial needs of seniors, baby boomers, and concerned children of elderly parents. In the process, he developed a new paradigm for understanding Medi-Cal eligibility rules and became a sought-after consultant on Medi-Cal to seniors and financial and legal advisors. Bob gained national prominence through articles in the *Los Angeles Times, Medical Economics, Financial Planning Magazine* and other publications. He maintains a busy financial planning and consulting practice in Upland, California.

The Technical Information:

Robert J. Cullen serves as president of Cullen Financial Services, Inc., a registered investment advisor. He is also branch manager for Linsco/Private Ledger, a national brokerage firm that serves independent financial advisors. Linsco/Private Ledger is a member of the National Association of Securities Dealers and Security Investor Protection Corporation.

ACKNOWLEDGEMENTS

AT THE ACADEMY AWARDS, winners bore audiences by thanking a long list of people who helped them achieve the golden statuette. I grudgingly recognize the need for these acknowledgements but silently wish I could skip ahead to the next presentation.

Since this is a book and not live TV, you, dear reader, may skip ahead to the next presentation. This section interests those people whose assistance so generously and importantly contributed to the completion of this book.

For their editorial insights, special thanks to Ken and Carole LaRue, Christina Stone and Chris Li.

For professional support and direction, special thanks to Nancy Langdon Jones.

For professional review and guidance, special thanks to F. Bentley Mooney.

For editing and rewriting, special thanks to Tinker Lindsay Beatty.

For cover design and book formatting, special thanks to Dotti Albertine.

For cover copy-editing and promotional text, special thanks to Laren Bright.

For shepherding this book and providing heart-felt moral support, special thanks to Ellen Reid.

For recording his wonderful CD *Romance*, special thanks to classical guitarist Michael Ryan. Michael, your music accompanied and inspired me through many writing sessions.

And for being wonderfully understanding of my compelling need to bring this book to completion and so, so forebearing of the many hours I was absent from home, extra special thanks to my wife, Elizabeth.

ELIZABETH, AGE 22

INTRODUCTION

WHEN SEVERE HEALTH CRISES STRIKE, consumers and their advisors understandably want assurance that an ill person's access to health care services is secured. They want answers to worst-case scenarios: "Must I spend myself into poverty to get help for my Alzheimer's-afflicted spouse?" "Will I be left to die if my health insurance runs out?"

This publication grew out of my work assisting families through health care crises with their disabled and elderly members. Often this work requires helping individuals become eligible for government-subsidized health care, known as Medi-Cal in California and Medicaid in the other 49 states.

For my work I developed *Put it in a Box*™ presentations that simplify the eligibility rules for obtaining Medi-Cal long-term care benefits. These *Put it in a Box*™ diagrams provide a new paradigm to understand Medi-Cal eligibility rules that will aid consumers and professional advisors–financial advisors, bankers, tax preparers, attorneys, social workers, nurses, care-givers–who serve disabled and elderly individuals.

Material in this book is arranged as a series of case studies that begin with a simple application for a single, elderly person with few assets and progresses to sophisticated planning for married couples with significant assets.

For people whose health and finances give them options, this book also provides guidance on avoiding Medi-Cal. Tightening federal and state budgets mean likely cuts in Medicaid/Medi-Cal funding in the future that will limit benefits for baby boomers. This book helps boomers examine long-term care planning options.

Finally this book ventures into the delicate, volatile area of family relations. When crises arise, will your family work in harmony or horror? This book provides the opportunity to measure your family ties quotient (FTQ) and anticipate family reactions before a crisis erupts. Steps taken now to remove emotional obstacles may smooth the road to better relations when family members most need support and consolation.

George with his 1933 Hudson

CHAPTER 1

GREAT UNCLE PAT

Our four choices for long-term care

GREAT UNCLE PAT WAS A TALL, SLENDER MAN who worked daily on the family farm in Northwest Iowa. He did not concern himself about long-term care issues or bad living habits. He drank whisky and beer, smoked cigars and cigarettes, and regularly ate beef and potatoes swimming in gravy. Whole milk and butter were also staples of his diet.

Great Uncle Pat was 92 years old when one November morning he complained of a terrible headache to Andy, his 88-year-old brother. In uncharacteristic fashion, Pat went back to bed instead of tending to the cattle in the barnyard.

Pat died that day. No hospitals. No emergency rooms. No nursing homes. Pat lived as he wanted, then passed on without fuss.

Great Uncle Pat's death epitomizes a 'good death,' a lucky fate shared by 10% of the American population. Unless we count suicide as an option, we mortal beings face four long-term choices as we contemplate the last years of our lives:

- Get lucky
- Enjoy your success
- Let someone else worry
- Let someone else pay

GET LUCKY

'Get lucky' was Great Uncle Pat's long-term care strategy. His planning can be summed in two words: Do nothing. The more hedonistic among us may label this as the "Eat, drink and be merry" strategy or its close cousin "Let tomorrow take care of itself."

Since this works for only 10% of the population, we have to ask ourselves: Do we feel lucky? Viewed realistically, we have nine-in-ten chances of needing some level of long-term care assistance during our lives.

Cultural factors play a role in long-term care planning. Caring for the elderly at home until they die is expected in some cultures. For these families, long-term care means unrelenting stress and backbreaking work for the next generation, usually a daughter or daughter-in-law.

Denial also plays a role in long-term care planning for many seniors. They know their time on Earth is limited; they know many people spend time in nursing homes; they know they should get their affairs in order. Yet many stubbornly ignore their children's and friends' entreaties to plan beforehand. Perhaps these seniors refuse to acknowledge their mortality because they fear such thinking will hasten their demise. Besides, didn't their great uncle drop dead one day without ever seeing the inside of a hospital or nursing home?

Denial also plays a role in long-term care planning for many seniors.

That you are reading this book is indication that 'Do Nothing' is not a comfortable choice for you.

ENJOY YOUR SUCCESS

For the fortunate few who enjoy great financial success, planning for long-term care is simply deciding which assets and/or income will be diverted to pay for necessary care when the need arises. To use an insurance industry description, these individuals may 'self insure' their risks of needing long-term care.

Interestingly, some wealthy people who can afford to self-insure purchase long-term care insurance. Anecdotal accounts from insurance sources indicate a desire by people of significant economic means to protect their asset base from potentially massive costs of extended long-term care.

LET SOMEONE ELSE WORRY

If 'Do Nothing' does not work for you and 'Enjoy Your Success' seems unlikely in this lifetime, then letting someone else worry for you may be your best choice.

You can transfer your long-term care worries from your shoulders onto the backs of insurance companies by purchasing stay-at-home-longer and protect-our-assets insurance. More commonly called long-term care insurance, this coverage provides income so you can stay home longer and protect your assets when serious medical conditions take away your ability to care for yourself or your spouse.

Obtaining this peace-of-mind coverage requires two critical ingredients: Reasonably healthy medical condition plus the financial wherewithal to pay for the insurance.

'Reasonably healthy medical condition' means you must qualify medically for coverage. Medical underwriting–when an insurance company examines your medical records–varies significantly among long-term care insurers. For example, where one company will reject automatically all applicants with any type of diabetes, another company will underwrite (provide coverage) for applicants with certain mild cases of diabetes.

Here is a commonsense rule of thumb: If you do not consider long-term care insurance until your doctor tells you about your serious illness, then you will likely not qualify for coverage. In other words, when you recognize that you REALLY need long-term coverage, you will likely NOT qualify to buy it.

If you qualify medically for this coverage, then you must consider if you qualify financially to pay for it. You need either surplus assets or surplus income to pay for this coverage. (A detailed discussion of long-term care insurance is featured later in this book in 'Peace of Mind Insurance.')

Ideally, everyone should make provisions for paying for long-term care, whether through self-insurance or purchased LTC coverage. Currently, Medicaid (Medi-Cal in California) pays for 60% of nursing home care in America. One needs only to consider the large numbers of baby boomers nearing their retirement years to recognize the improbability of our federal and state treasuries continuing to pay 60% of nursing home care indefinitely.

LET SOMEONE ELSE PAY

Medi-Cal is the payer of last resort for individuals who lack means to pay privately for medical care. Medi-Cal is a means-tested program, which means an individual or a couple must meet certain asset requirements to qualify for benefits. Additionally, the individual may be required to pay some or most of his/her monthly income to the nursing home as his/her designated co-payment or share of cost.

The following chapters simplify Medi-Cal long-term care so consumers and their advisors better understand available programs. We begin with a simple case where we seek benefits for an elderly Grandmother.

LEFT: DAVID, AGE 2
RIGHT: MICHAEL, AGE 10

Florence and Joe, 1997

CHAPTER 2

GRANDMOTHER

When income does not count as an asset

FOR YOUR GRANDMOTHER TO QUALIFY for Medi-Cal benefits for her nursing home care, her end-of-month bank balance must be under $2,000. She must also be over age 65, or blind, or disabled, and have a medical need for nursing home care. You receive her latest bank statement and your stomach knots when you see an ending balance of $2,800. “Blast it!” you mutter: “Now she won’t qualify and I’ll have to pay the nursing home out of my pocket!”

Maybe not. Think about this: when you balance your checkbook, do you accept the balance printed on your statement as the current balance in your check register? Probably not, since you likely wrote checks during the period between the closing date of the bank balance and the date you balance your checkbook.

Medi-Cal determines eligibility from month to month. If Grandmother qualifies for benefits on the last day of the month, she qualifies for the entire month. Now consider your Grandmother’s checking account. Suppose you wrote checks for $300 on her account during the *month of application* that were not posted to the account by the last day of the month. Subtracting these outstanding checks of $300 from $2,800 brings her closing balance to $2,500.

"So what?" you reply: "She still has more than $2,000. She has too much money to qualify."

Maybe not. Grandmother receives $820 each month from social security. She also receives $180 pension income every month. Here is an important and often overlooked fact about Medi-Cal eligibility requirements: **Income does not count as an asset in the month of receipt; income becomes an asset the month after it is received.** Therefore, to calculate Grandmother's *non-exempt countable resources* for any month, her income received *that* month must be deducted from the balance.

Grandmother's non-exempt countable resources are calculated thusly:

End of month bank balance	$2,800
Outstanding same-month checks	(300)
Income received during month	(1,000)
Total non-exempt countable resources	$1,500

Voila! Her assets are below $2,000. Grandmother qualifies. Your worries are over.

Maybe not. My first appeal of a Medi-Cal denial of benefits featured miscalculation of a checking account end-of-month balance by a county eligibility worker. When I called her supervisor, I received the same answer: Your client is *over-property.*

When my client heard of the denial of benefits, she was upset and mistrustful of my assurances that Medi-Cal was wrong and I was right. I filled out the back of the denial notice and filed an appeal. I began researching regulations and sought counsel from my informal network of Medi-Cal consultants and attorneys to prepare for a hearing before an administrative law judge.

The case never reached the hearing level. I received a call from a county appeals specialist to discuss the case. When I explained the calculation errors of the eligibility worker and her supervisor, the appeals specialist asked if I would agree to a *conditional withdrawal* of my hearing request. If I agreed to withdraw my appeal request, the specialist would send the case back to the field office for re-processing. I was not relinquishing any of my client's rights to appeal. I was simply giving Medi-Cal a second chance to get it right.

I agreed to withdraw my hearing request. The case was sent back to the field office. Shortly thereafter my client received a *Notice of Action* stating her application for benefits had been approved.

Medi-Cal operates under regulations and rules that often confuse consumers and professionals. Standard rules that apply in other areas of taxes, finances and law often are often disregarded under Medi-Cal regulations.

For example, many California residents know we live in a community property state, where property acquired during a marriage is deemed owned equally. An exception to this rule concerns inheritances. A married person may keep an inheritance as 'separate property,' distinct from the family's community property. This distinction is disregarded by Medi-Cal. If a married woman has $100,000 of inheritance owned as her separate property, her inheritance is counted with the family's community property when applying for Medi-Cal benefits for her husband.

Another example concerns transfers of *exempt* and *non-exempt resources*. Medi-Cal is a means-tested program, so you can't give money away and then qualify for benefits. Medi-Cal assesses penalty periods that start with the date of the transfer and continue for a period of time commensurate with the size of the gift. The larger the gift, the longer the penalty period. This makes sense.

However, where logic breaks down concerns the distinction Medi-Cal makes between transfers of exempt and non-exempt resources. As explained in later chapters, a home is usually an exempt asset. Cash is typically a non-exempt resource when held outside of pension plans, such as IRAs.

Let's assume your Grandmother owns a house that she bought for $30,000 over 30 years ago and now it's worth $300,000. If she gives this house away, you would expect that she would be ineligible for Medi-Cal for a long period, yes? However, in the often-illogical world of Medi-Cal, Grandmother can qualify for Medi-Cal benefits and then transfer her house away and still maintain her benefits. No penalty is assessed for transferring her home away, *if done according to Medi-Cal rules*. However, if Grandmother sells her house for $300,000 and gives away the non-exempt cash, her benefits will be terminated. Giving away $300,000 cash disqualifies her for Medi-Cal benefits, but giving away her $300,000 house has no effect on her continued eligibility.

Medi-Cal does not fit into any normal business, financial or legal paradigm. Accept that you need to adjust your thinking whenever dealing with Medi-Cal and this book will make more sense to you.

(Note: Asset transfers involve complicated ethical, legal and financial considerations. Further discussion about transfers is featured in "Legitimate transfers." Seek professional assistance before making any transfers.)

CHAPTER 3

GRANDMOTHER, PART II

Put it in a Box™ to gain eligibility

GRANDMOTHER'S HEALTH CRISIS started when she suffered a medical emergency at her home. Her neighbor called 9-1-1 and she was transported by ambulance to the nearest hospital. She stayed in the hospital until she was stabilized and transferred to a *skilled nursing facility*. Because she receives social security, Grandmother has *Medicare* as her primary health insurance. She also has *Medicare supplemental insurance* to pay most costs not covered by Medicare. This combined coverage has paid for her medical expenses so far, but you have been notified that her Medicare skilled nursing benefit will likely end soon (most people do not receive their full 100 days of skilled nursing benefit) and Grandmother will be reclassified as a custodial care patient. The social worker, an employee of the skilled nursing facility, wants to know what you want to do.

At the point where seniors are classified as custodial care patients, their families face four options: 1) take the patient home and pay for expensive in-home care at costs ranging from $14 to $25 per hour; 2) if the medical condition allows, transfer to a lower *level of care,* such as *assisted living* or *board and care,* which range in cost from $1,200 to $5,000 per month; 3) pay privately for continued care in a facility as a custodial care patient at costs ranging from $3,500 to $7,000 per month; 4) qualify for Medi-Cal to pay for custodial care room and board.

In this case, qualifying Grandmother for Medi-Cal benefits is the only viable option as she and her family members lack resources for her to receive in-home care or pay for a lower level of care.

Finding a bed in a Medi-Cal certified custodial care facility for Grandmother will be the first challenge. Nursing homes prefer private pay patients because facilities typically charge more per month for private pay patients than they receive from Medi-Cal for providing similar care to Medi-Cal patients.

Are nursing homes allowed to discriminate against Medi-Cal patients? No, they are not supposed to discriminate. For example, a facility is not supposed to designate a certain number of beds as "Medi-Cal beds." If a nursing home is *Medi-Cal certified,* i.e., certified to participate in the Medi-Cal program, a resident eligible for Medi-Cal may reside in any bed in the nursing home.

Additionally, a nursing home cannot require that a resident certify that he or she is not eligible for Medi-Cal benefits. Nor can they require assurances or guarantees that a resident will not later apply for Medi-Cal benefits.

However, in spite of these legal prohibitions, families daily encounter obstacles to admission when they admit upfront that they need Medi-Cal benefits for a loved one.

In Grandmother's case, if you tell a nursing home representative that she will need Medi-Cal, your prospects for placing her in that facility may diminish. You may be told "We can place your grandmother's name on our Medi-Cal waiting list." However, if you have your checkbook ready to write a check to the facility for the first one to two months' care, you may find that a bed becomes available sooner.

So what happens if you place your grandmother as a private pay patient and then apply for Medi-Cal? First of all, the facility–because it is Medi-Cal certified–can't evict your grandmother. Her level of care should not change, though it is commonplace to see patients transferred from single-bed rooms to two-bed and three-bed rooms when they change from private pay to Medi-Cal pay status. You can challenge this move since they are not allowed to discriminate.

Remember: When you pay attention to your loved one, so will the staff.

Should you fight a bed change? This is very difficult to answer. Will you win the battle and lose the war? One never knows. Regardless if your grandmother is private pay or Medi-Cal, her quality of care will depend significantly on this important fact: Patients with regular, attentive visitors receive better care.

If Grandmother needs help eating, be there at lunchtime. If you know the facility runs short of staff during certain times of day, make it a point to be there to help out. If you can't visit regularly, hire someone, such as a visiting nurse, to check on her. Vary your visiting times so you are not too predictable. Be friendly to all of the staff but also advocate firmly for your loved one when things go awry. Remember: When you pay attention to your loved one, so will the staff.

ELIGIBILITY REQUIREMENTS

Does Grandmother qualify for Medi-Cal long-term benefits? Let's look at Graphic S1. Any assets that fit within a box are protected, i.e., exempt for Medi-Cal qualifying purposes. The boxed assets are labeled by Medi-Cal as *exempt resources.*

Your Grandmother has these assets:

- A two-bedroom, single-family home with no mortgage and miniscule property taxes because of Proposition 13 protections;
- A ten-year-old car with 28,000 miles;
- $5,000 of group term life insurance through her pension;
- Pre-paid burial plot at a nearby cemetery;
- No IRAs or other qualified pension plans;
- $11,000 in a bank checking account.

Her monthly income totals $1,000, with $880 coming from social security and $120 from her pension. Interest income from her checking account is minimal.

Using Graphic S1, we put her assets into their appropriate boxes. Into the first box goes her house. On the Medi-Cal application is a question: "Does the applicant intend to return home?" Always answer this question 'yes.' Whether she has any real prospects for returning home is irrelevant. You are acting on her behalf, and if she could, she would go home. Indicating her intent to go home makes her residence an exempt asset.

The definition of an exempt residence is not limited to a house or mobile home. For example, if Grandma resides in one unit of a four-plex that she owns, the entire four-plex is considered her exempt residence. This exemption applies only for eligibility; after she dies, her residence may be subject to recovery, which is discussed later.

$$ Put it in a Box™ Graphic S1

ASSETS — Single Person's → Grandmom's assets

RESIDENCE	VEHICLE	TERM LIFE INSURANCE	BURIAL	IRA	PROPERTY RESERVE
Single-family home, no mortgage	Automobile	$5,000	One plot	None	$2,000

NON-EXEMPT RESOURCES

Bank accounts, CDs	$ 11,000
Additional vehicles (Kelly Blue Book value)	
Cash value life insurance (cash surrender value)	
Rental real estate (assessed value, not FMV)	
Investment accounts (stocks, bonds, etc.)	
OTHER	
TOTAL	$ 11,000
Subtract $2,000 Property Reserve	(2,000)
Excess non-exempt resources	$ 9,000

Over property

INCOME

Social security	$ 880
Pension	$ 120
IRA Income	
Total	$ 1,000
Less maintenance need	$ (35)
Share of cost	$ 965

The second box shelters her car. No dollar limit is set for a vehicle.

Into the third box goes her $5,000 group term life insurance. Because it has no cash value, i.e., she must die before anyone can claim any benefits, this is labeled as an exempt resource.

A small amount of cash value life insurance may be exempt, if the total death benefit of all cash value policies is $1,500 or less.

This brings us to the fourth box, Burial. You can spend any amount of money on burial arrangements provided there are no refunds after the person is buried. If burial arrangements are irrevocable, they meet Medi-Cal requirements and are exempted. Mortuary representatives know how to handle such arrangements when you inform them that you will be applying for Medi-Cal benefits.

Grandmother has no individual retirement accounts (IRA) nor any other cash-balance pension plans, so her IRA box is empty.

The last box is her $2,000 property reserve. I recommend keeping $1,900 in a checking account as a patient's 'running balance,' i.e., the end-of-the-month balance after subtracting outstanding checks and income received during the month.

Medi-Cal also permits establishment of a designated burial account of $1,500. This can be set up as a savings account at a bank. A joint owner may be placed on the account. When Grandmother dies, these assets are to be used for burial purposes.

OVER PROPERTY

After putting Grandmother's assets into appropriate exempt

resource boxes, we see she has $9,000 left outside of a box. In Medi-Cal terms, she is $9,000 *over property.* If you go to Medi-Cal and apply for benefits for her, the eligibility worker will tell you that you have until the end of the month of application to *spend down* her non-exempt resources, which in this case total $9,000. Besides paying privately for her care, what can you do to make her eligible?

Put it in a Box™. That's right, look for ways to move the non-exempt resources into an exempt resource box. Here are useful items to consider:

Business property can be exempted in some instances. Equipment and inventory that is used for employment or business may be exempted if valid business use can be proven. Note: Rental real estate is generally not exempted as business property.

Does Grandmother's house need repairs? Ideally, repairs should be completed by month's end to keep accounting simple for the Medi-Cal eligibility worker. However significant house repairs involve contractors, bids, delays, etc., and typically require weeks to complete. This delays can be handled by getting written bids and contracts for the repair work and placing funds specifically for these tasks in an escrow account. In Grandmother's case, you have time to get sprinklers installed in her back yard and the wooden fence along the back property line repaired by the end of the month of application. Document all spending with bids, checks and receipts.

Pre-pay Grandmother's burial expenses. Currently, your grandmother owns a lot next to her husband. She wants a modest funeral and burial in a casket. Pre-paying burial expenses can easily use up $4,500. Tell the mortuary representative that you are applying for Medi-Cal and need the arrangements to be irrevocable.

Other options to achieve eligibility include upgrading her vehicle and gifting. These strategies are discussed later.

Graphic S2 shows the changes. Everything fits into a box and Grandmother will qualify for Medi-Cal. Provide all verifications requested by the eligibility worker and soon Grandmother will receive a *Notice of Action* stating she has been approved for benefits. The notice will also list her *share of cost* that must be paid each month to the nursing home to maintain her eligibility.

SHARE OF COST

Share of cost is the co-payment Medi-Cal applicants must pay from their income to remain eligible for benefits. An individual is allowed to keep $35 per month for incidental costs. The remaining income goes to Medi-Cal on a monthly basis.

Grandmother has the option to keep or drop her Medicare supplemental insurance. If she keeps her coverage, Medi-Cal will allow the premiums to be paid from her share of cost.

In Grandmother's situation, the mechanics of paying share of cost work this way. Medi-Cal issues a Notice of Action to your grandmother stating she is eligible for benefits and listing her share of cost. The nursing facility also receives notice of her eligibility, so they also know her share of cost.

$$ Put it in a Box™ Graphic S2

ASSETS — Single Person's → Grandmom's assets

RESIDENCE	VEHICLE	TERM LIFE INSURANCE	BURIAL	IRA	PROPERTY RESERVE
Single-family home, no mortgage $4,500 repairs	Automobile	$5,000	One plot Irrevocable arrangements $4,500	None	$2,000

NON-EXEMPT RESOURCES

Bank accounts, CDs	$ 11,000
Additional vehicles (Kelly Blue Book value)	
Cash value life insurance (cash surrender value)	
Rental real estate (assessed value, not FMV)	
Investment accounts (stocks, bonds, etc.)	
OTHER	
TOTAL	$ 11,000
Subtract $2,000 Property Reserve	(2,000)
House repairs	(4,500)
Pre-need Burial	(4,500)
Excess non-exempt resources	$ 0

INCOME

Social security	$ 880
Pension	$ 120
IRA Income	
Total	$ 1,000
Less maintenance need	$ (35)
Share of cost	$ 965

Several months before she became ill, Grandmother added your name to her checking account, so you have authority to write checks on her account. At the beginning of each month, she receives in her checking account her social security and pension payments. This will raisc her account balance over $2,000. However, that is not a problem. Each month you will write a check to the nursing home for her share of cost and her bank balance will drop back below $2,000 by month's end.

You want to keep the 'running balance' of Grandmother's checking account below $1,900. If the balance begins to come close to $2,000 due to the $35 she keeps each month, then use funds to buy her some new clothes, have her hair done, etc. Spend the money for her benefit and keep receipts to verify your actions.

Many people believe that Grandmother's social security and pension **must** be assigned to the nursing home. Such assignment is not mandatory. However, this is an option that can simplify monthly procedures for meeting Grandmother's share of cost. The nursing facility will establish a trust account to receive her income and hold her monthly $35 incidentals allowance.

Should Grandmother's financial situation change, e.g., her income increases or decreases, she or her representatives are required to notify Medi-Cal within 10 days of the change. During the application process you will have signed disclosure forms that spell out this requirement, so it is useless to plead ignorance about it.

One change of income you will likely see (and not have to report): Medi-Cal will begin paying her Medicare Part B premium. This typically occurs two to three months after she is declared eligible. Her social security payments and her share of cost will increase by a commensurate amount. A Notice of Action will be issued showing the new share of cost, which must be paid to the nursing home each month.

REDETERMINATION OF BENEFITS

About four to six weeks before the anniversary of filing for benefits for your Grandmother, the Medi-Cal office will send out redetermination papers. Sometimes these papers are sent to the nursing home. Too often, they are left on Grandmother's bedside table and subsequently disappear, so it is good idea to alert the nursing home to their anticipated arrival. You may want to put a note on your calendar to remind the nursing home staff about her incoming mail about one month before the anniversary date of her original filing for benefits.

Some counties have streamlined the redetermination process by requiring verifications only for assets and income that have changed since eligibility was established.

Redetermination is a formal process whereby Medi-Cal annually rechecks your Grandmother's finances to determine her continued eligibility for benefits. Medi-Cal wants to know if her bank balance is still below $2,000 and whether her income has increased. Complete the forms, provide verifications of her assets and income and her eligibility for benefits will continue for another year.

RECOVERY AFTER HER DEATH

So far we have discussed making Grandmother eligible for benefits and maintaining her eligibility by paying her share of cost. A third aspect of receiving Medi-Cal assistance involves *Recovery.*

The California Department of Health Services is required to seek recovery for payments made to nursing homes from the estates of deceased Medi-Cal recipients. Under current regulations, if nothing remains in Grandmother's estate except her checking account with less than $2,000, then this account is all there is left from which the State can recover its payments.

The key phrase in the above paragraph is 'under current regulations.' A key objective of this book is to alert consumers to Medi-Cal issues where professional assistance is warranted. If your Grandmother is not concerned about passing any of her assets to the next generation or she believes the State should be repaid for payments made for her care, then Recovery will not be a concern for her. However, if avoiding Recovery is important to Grandmother, then it is paramount to seek professional assistance. Such assistance is especially warranted if Grandmother wants to preserve her residence for beneficiaries.

. . . if avoiding Recovery is important to Grandmother, then it is paramount to seek professional assistance.

In general, seek competent professional guidance for any recovery issues.

CHAPTER 4

MOTHER
Evaluating options for Mother's care

USING THE *PUT IT IN A BOX*™ CONCEPT, let's examine a more complicated situation involving a single person. This time you are assisting your mother, age 78, who has these assets:

- Two-bedroom condominium, estimated value $220,000, with a $20,000 mortgage
- 1989 Cadillac with 95,000 miles
- $10,000 group term life insurance
- No burial pre-arrangements
- Individual retirement account (IRA) with $40,000 invested in stocks and bonds
- Individual retirement account (IRA) with $15,000 invested in a fixed annuity
- $60,000 in CDs, soonest maturing in three months
- $10,000 in her checking account

For income, Mom has a pension from California State Teachers Retirement System (STRS) that pays $1,200 and social security of $440, both paid monthly. Since she is past age 70½, she must meet IRS rules for required minimum distributions from her IRAs. Presently, she takes these required

required withdrawals as an annual distribution of $2,400 from only one account, as allowed by the IRS.

PUT IT IN A BOX™

We slot Mom's exempt resources into their proper boxes (Graphic S3). We see she has $68,000 of non-exempt resources. By looking at *Income* on the lower half of S3, we see she will have a monthly share of cost totaling $1,805.

Several factors need to be considered:

(1) Since the monthly cost of placing Mom on Medi-Cal in a nursing home is going to be over $1,800 in share-of-cost payments, other care options should be considered. For example, could Mom reside at a lower, less-costly level of care, such as a board and care, where her surroundings will be less institutional? Let's assume you could find an attractive board and care (many are converted homes that take four to six patients) that costs $2,500 per month. Adding $300 monthly for drugs and other costs brings her costs of care to $2,800 per month or $33,600 annually. She receives annual income of $22,080. This leaves an annual shortfall of $11,520. Mom has $70,000 in her bank accounts. At an annual withdrawal rate of $11,520, these funds would pay for Mom's care for six years.

(2) You could help Mom live at home with daily in-home care. At $15 per hour for 10 hours of care six days per week (you provide care for one day per week), her care will cost about $54,000 annually. Her income plus her $70,000 would fund this care situation for about two years.

$$ Put it in a Box™ — Graphic S3

ASSETS — Single Person's → Mom's assets

Residence	Vehicle	Term Life Insurance	Burial	IRA	Property Reserve
2-bdrm condo FMV $220K Mort $20K	1989 Cadillac	$10,000	None	$40K in stocks and bonds, $15K in a fixed annuity, $200 monthly income	$2,000

NON-EXEMPT RESOURCES

Bank accounts, CDs	$ 70,000
Additional vehicles (Kelly Blue Book value)	
Cash value life insurance (cash surrender value)	
Rental real estate (assessed value, not FMV)	
Investment accounts (stocks, bonds, etc.)	
Other	
Total	$ 70,000
Subtract $2,000 Property Reserve	(2,000)
Excess non-exempt resources	$ 68,000

Over property

INCOME

Social security	$ 440
Pension	$ 1,200
IRA Income	200
Total	$ 1,840
Less maintenance need	$ (35)
Share of cost	$ 1,805

(3) With her $1,800+ monthly income and $70,000 in the bank, Mom could pay privately for her care in a single-bed room for two to three years. Very few patients remain in a nursing home for more than two years. Either the patient gets better and goes home or the patient does not get better and goes to heaven. If Mom remains in a nursing home after she has exhausted her bank funds, she could apply for Medi-Cal benefits and pursue strategies that would allow her to preserve for her children the equity in her home, which at $200,000 is by far her most valuable asset.

I raise these points to encourage families to think more broadly for care solutions than simply "We must place Mom in a nursing home and qualify for Medi-Cal." Not only may you find more loving care solutions for your mother, you may also avoid the entire ordeal of dealing with Medi-Cal eligibility, redeterminations and post-death recovery.

However, if nursing home care is required for Mom at this stage and Medi-Cal eligibility is desired, what are workable strategies to achieve eligibility?

First, focus on costs that are certain to occur in the future. In Mom's case, she has not completed any burial arrangements. Using $5,000 to $7,000 to prepay irrevocable burial arrangements is sound fiscal policy. This action moves funds from non-exempt to exempt status.

Paying off Mom's mortgage makes sense. Upgrading a residence with new applicances, carpet and paint are also sensible and acceptable ways to add value to Mom's holdings and move non-exempt resources to exempt status.

Consider pre-paying ongoing expenses that can't be paid out of Mom's income once she qualifies for Medi-Cal, such as condominium homeowner association dues for her residence. Unless a doctor will state in writing that Mom is likely to return home within six months, Medi-Cal does not make allowance for Mom to pay housing costs out of her income. Mobile home space rent monthly fees also fit into this category.

Renting out a mobile home is often not allowed by mobile home parks. If renting is allowed, rent payments will cover space rent fees.

Converting Mom's condo to a rental unit will provide income to pay association dues and other upkeep. The net income from the rental will be added to Mom's income and thereby increase her share of cost. The rental agreement needs to have provisions stating Mom is allowed to re-occupy her home should she recover her health. Inquire of the Medi-Cal eligibility worker handling her application how that specific Medi-Cal office handles exempt residence rentals and tailor the rental agreement accordingly.

After careful consideration, you decide on this plan:

Mom's non-exempt resources	$ 70,000
Fund property reserve	(2,000)
Prepay burial arrangements	(5,000)
Pay off mortgage	(20,000)
Install new carpet	(7,000)
Non-exempt resources remaining	$ 36,000

You could upgrade Mom's vehicle. You may ask, "How can we do that? Mom can't drive." My reply: "There you go again, trying to be logical." The fact that Mom can't drive has no bearing on the status of her exempt vehicle.

Gifting some of Mom's assets is also an option that comes with attendant restrictions and dangers. See "Legitimate transfers."

Theoretically–until Medi-Cal institutes a dollar limit on the value of an exempt vehicle–you could use all of Mom's non-exempt resources to buy a sleek luxury car. For ethical reasons alone I don't recommend that strategy. But also for practical reasons I don't recommend outrageous strategies. (See "Eligibility Workers have feelings, too.")

However, upgrading Mom's vehicle to something reasonable that can be used to transport her to doctors' visits makes sense. You will need to place someone else's name on second position on the title of the car so you can insure it.

Spending $26,000 for a newer vehicle would lower Mom's non-exempt resource assets to $10,000. These remaining funds can be used to place Mom in a facility and pay for the first month or two of care.

Here's our final calculation:

Mom's non-exempt resources	$ 70,000
Fund property reserve	(2,000)
Prepay burial arrangements	(5,000)
Pay off mortgage	(20,000)
Install new carpet	(7,000)
Trade-in old car, buy newer vehicle	(26,000)
Non-exempt resources remaining	$ 10,000

Graphic S4 shows the final effect.

$$ Put it in a Box™ — Graphic S4

ASSETS — Single Person's → Mom's assets

Residence	Vehicle	Term Life Insurance	Burial	IRA	Property Reserve
2-bdrm condo FMV $220K Mort $20K $20,000 $7,000	1989 Cadillac sold $26K for new car	$10,000	One plot $5K for pre-burial	$40K in stocks and bonds, in a fixed annuity, $200 monthly income	$2,000

NON-EXEMPT RESOURCES

Bank accounts, CDs	$ 70,000
Additional vehicles (Kelly Blue Book value)	
Cash value life insurance (cash surrender value)	
Rental real estate (assessed value, not FMV)	
Investment accounts (stocks, bonds, etc.)	
Other	
Total	$ 70,000
Subtract $2,000 Property Reserve	(2,000)
Pay off mortgage	(20,000)
New carpet	(7,000)
Newer car	(26,000)
Pre-need Burial	(5,000)
Excess non-exempt resources	$ 10,000

INCOME

Social security	$ 440
Pension	$ 1,200
IRA Income	200
Total	$ 1,840
Less maintenance need	$ (35)
Share of cost	$ 1,805

POSSIBLE PROCESSING PROBLEMS

Though Mom's IRAs meet IRS and Medi-Cal standards and should be exempted without question, they may cause processing problems. Eligibility workers like to see IRAs fit these rules:

Is each IRA making distributions of principal and income?
Is each IRA paying monthly distributions?
Is the IRA/annuity annuitized?

Medi-Cal offices are notorious for denying cases incorrectly because of misapplied IRA regulations. Why? For years the regulations for handling IRAs and other qualified pension plans were unclear. In 2002, Medi-Cal authorities at the state level issued All County Welfare Directors Letter No.: 02-51. The goal of this ACWD is stated in the first paragraph:

The purpose of this letter is to provide counties with information regarding the treatment of work-related pension funds, IRA's, Keogh's and other work-related retirement funds under IRS Code in determining Medi-Cal eligibility.

The full text of this All County letter may be downloaded from our website www.savingmomanddad.com. Here are the relevant rules for Mom's IRAs as stipulated in ACWD Letter No.: 02-51:

Eligibility workers (EWs) should not second-guess distributions from IRAs, especially for applicants who have reached age 70½. EWs are directed to accept the amount reported by over age 70½ applicants as meeting Medi-Cal requirements. For applicants below age 70½, EWs are directed to obtain verification from the IRA custodian or financial broker that the distributions correspond to IRS life expectancy requirements.

An applicant does not have to take distributions from each IRA. Once the required minimum distribution (RMD) is established for all work-related pension plans, IRS regulations state that the RMD may be withdrawn from only one IRA to exempt all IRAs owned by the applicant.

Neither Medi-Cal nor IRS regulations require that IRA distributions be taken monthly. However, if IRA distributions are taken as an annual lump sum, the payment is considered income during the month of receipt and property after the month of receipt. This routinely confuses everyone. Make your life easier: have Mom's IRAs pay monthly distributions. If the financial institution holding Mom's IRAs does not cooperate, consider transferring Mom's IRAs to a more cooperative institution.

IRAs that involve annuities especially confuse eligibility workers. The EW may state that your Mom is required to annuitize her IRA annuity. This is not required and is addressed in ACWD 02-51. If the EW and the Supervisor insist that the IRA annuity must be annuitized even after you have steered them towards ACWD 02-51, tell the EW and Supervisor that you will file an appeal if they issue a denial based on their erroneous information. Get competent professional help and you should win the appeal.

WAITING FOR ELIGIBILITY

How long does Medi-Cal take to process an application? Medi-Cal is required to act on the application within 45 days in the absence of an agreement with the applicant to extend the time. The LTC facility must wait for the county action and may not require more than the estimated share of cost from the applicant or applicant's spouse. Medi-Cal payment–once the application is approved–is made retroactively to the first day of the month in which the application is received.

HELPFUL FACTS

Applicants may apply for up to three months of retroactive benefits. However, this is useful only if an applicant can prove eligibility for those prior months.

Unpaid medical bills incurred before an individual achieves Medi-Cal eligibility may be used to offset share of cost under the *Hunt vs. Kizer* program. (See "Eligibility Workers have feelings, too" for more information about *Hunt vs. Kizer.*)

FRANK AND YVONNE, JUNE 20, 1959

CHAPTER 5

DAD AND MOM

Generous provisions for married couples

SINGLE PERSONS OFTEN COMPLAIN that our society favors married couples. This complaint holds true with Medi-Cal. Married couples have much greater flexibility than single persons to preserve assets and income and qualify one spouse for long-term benefits.

Let's begin by examining Graphic M1, *Put it in a Box*™–'Married couple, one person in long-term care.' A large box placed in a second row and labeled *Community Spouse Resource Allowance (CSRA)* is added to the six boxes featured for a single person. As indicated on the graphic, the CSRA 2004 limit is $92,760. These are assets that a Well Spouse is allowed to keep in addition to the assets allowed for the Ill Spouse.

Let's consider a sample case. Your father, 71, went to the hospital with a broken hip. After using 20 days of Medicare Skilled Nursing Benefit, he has been notified that he will be reclassified as a custodial care patient. Your mother, 69, is not strong enough to care for him at home so she is faced with two choices: paying privately for his care in the nursing home at $4,500 per month or qualifying him for Medi-Cal benefits.

These are your parents' assets:

- Single-family home in good condition, no mortgage
- Two vehicles: 1999 Lexus RX300 and 1995 Honda Accord
- Whole life insurance on Dad, $40,000 death benefit, $4,760 cash value
- Two burial plots
- IRA owned by Dad, $60,000 balance, taking $200 monthly distributions
- IRA owned by Mom, $20,000 balance, taking no distributions
- $50,000 in CDs
- Checking account $10,000
- $31,000 in stocks and bonds

Your parents' income:

- Dad receives $1,200 social security, Mom receives $550
- Dad receives $600 from a pension, plus $200 monthly from his IRA
- Together they receive $200 per month investment income.

Put it in a Box™. After slotting your parents' exempt and non-exempt resources, we see they have $6,000 of excess non-exempt resources remaining. Your parents want to keep their two vehicles and life insurance. They also prefer not to withdraw their CDs early and incur early-withdrawal penalties.

This case offers a simple, sensible solution. Dad and Mom have two burial plots but they have not pre-paid their burial expenses. Using at least $6,000 to pre-pay their burial expenses will lower their non-exempt resources to the $92,760

$$ Put it in a Box™ — Graphic M1

ASSETS — Married Couple, one person in long-term care

RESIDENCE	VEHICLE	TERM LIFE INSURANCE	BURIAL	IRA	PROPERTY RESERVE
Single-family home, no mortgage	Lexus	None	Two plots	$60K - Dad $200 monthly income $20K - Mom No income	$2,000

Community Spouse Resource Allowance (CSRA)

2004 = $92,760

NON-EXEMPT RESOURCES

Checking and savings accounts	$ 10,000
Certificates of deposit (CDs)	50,000
Additional Vehicles	5,000
Cash value life insurance	4,760
Rental real estate (assessed value)	
Investment accounts	31,000
Any other assests	
TOTAL	$ 100,760
Property Reserve	(2,000)
CSRA (2004 limit)	$ (92,760)
Excess non-exempt resources	$ 6,000

$92,760 ← CSRA (2004 limit)

INCOME

	His	Hers
Social security	$ 1,200	$ 550
Pension	$ 600	
IRA Income	$ 200	
Investment income	$ 100	$ 100
Total	$ 2,100	$ 650

Minimum Monthly Maintenance Needs Allowance (MMMNA)
2004 limit = $2,319

I am amazed when clients who would never dream of committing criminal acts lose their heads when it comes to Medi-Cal.

A typical comment: "I knew Mom could only have $2,000 so I cleaned out her checking account."

If Mom is suddenly broke, you think an eligibility worker might smell a problem? Medi-Cal computers connect to IRS and other government databanks. It is not difficult for them to trace bank accounts.

Hiding money from Medi-Cal is a criminal act. You wouldn't think of shoplifting or committing armed robbery, yet defrauding Medi-Cal can just as easily land you in jail.

limit. The remainder of their non-exempt resources can be sheltered as part of Mom's Community Spousc Resource Allowance.

For income, Mom will receive allocation from Dad to bring her income to the Minimum Monthly Maintenance Needs Allowance (MMMNA). The remainder of Dad's income will go the nursing home as his share of cost. Graphic M2 shows the changes to assets and income for Dad and Mom.

POTENTIAL PROCESSING PROBLEMS

Dad's and Mom's IRAs are correctly situated to meet Medi-Cal regulations. However, uninformed EWs may assert that Mom's IRA must be paying income. This is not required for any qualified pension

$$ Put it in a Box™ Graphic M2

ASSETS — Married Couple, one person in long-term care

RESIDENCE	VEHICLE	TERM LIFE INSURANCE	BURIAL	IRA	PROPERTY RESERVE
Single-family home, no mortgage	Lexus	None	$6K for pre-need burial	$60K - Dad $200 monthly income $20K - Mom No income	$2,000

Community Spouse Resource Allowance (CSRA)	NON-EXEMPT RESOURCES	
2004 = $92,760	Checking and savings accounts	$ 10,000
	Certificates of deposit (CDs)	50,000
	Additional Vehicles	5,000
	Cash value life insurance	4,760
	Rental real estate (assessed value)	
	Investment accounts	31,000
	Any other assests	
	TOTAL	$ 100,760
	Property Reserve	(2,000)
	Pre-need burial	(6,000)
$92,760 ←	CSRA (2004 limit)	$ (92,760)
	Excess non-exempt resources	$ 0

INCOME

	His	Hers
Social security	$ 1,200	$ 550
Pension	$ 600	
IRA Income	$ 200	
Investment income	$ 100	$ 100
Total	$ 2,100	$ 650
Maintenance need	$ (35)	
Allocation	$(1,669) →	1,669
Share of cost	$ 396	
Well spouse monthly income		$ 2,319 ← MMMNA

Minimum Monthly Maintenance Needs Allowance (MMMNA) 2004 limit = $2,319 accounts of the Well Spouse. If you encounter this problem, I recommend steering the eligibility worker to All County Welfare Directors Letter No. 02-51. If the worker and supervisor persist on denying the case after you have supplied them this information, ask to speak to the unit or district manager. If necessary, get professional assistance and appeal the denial.

To obtain verification of Dad's cash value life insurance, contact the insurance company and request they send a statement of policy values to the address of record. Normally insurance company customer service representatives will cooperate with this request if the statement is sent to the address of record.

Once eligibility is achieved, your parents will have 90 days to transfer non-exempt assets into Mom's name. Your Dad can only have $2,000 of non-exempt resources in his name. Since Dad's life insurance has cash value over $2,000, the policy's ownership will need to be transferred out of his name. If he is legally competent to sign forms, your Dad can transfer ownership to Mom. If he is not legally competent, then you need a valid power of attorney or other legal authority to make insurance transfers.

Families often encounter problems when they take a durable power of attorney to a bank. Banks do not like durable power of attorney documents drafted by estate planning attorneys. The banks, especially the biggest ones, tell consumers they will only accept power of attorney documents that were drafted by the bank. Elder law attorneys can often force banks to honor a valid, non-bank specific durable power of attorney, however, doing so takes time and incurs attorney fees. This problem can be avoided if individuals execute beforehand bank-specific power of attorney forms as well as durable power of attorney forms drafted by an estate planning attorney.

When you have completed transferring non-exempt assets from Dad to Mom, send copies of new bank accounts and any other necessary financial statements directly to Medi-Cal to show your parents have met the 90-day requirement. If special circumstances–such as having to get court approval to change ownership–delays this process beyond 90 days, request an extension.

DAD AND MOM, PART II

Let's give Dad and Mom more assets and see how we gain eligibility with a more complicated case.

- They own and rent out the first house that they purchased in 1959 for $18,000. This rental property has a fair market value of $250,000 and an assessed value of $36,000. They net $600 per month income from this asset.
- They have a portfolio of telephone stocks, begun with an original purchase of 200 shares of AT&T in 1978. Following the breakup of Ma Bell and subsequent mergers and spin-offs, they have a portfolio of telecom stocks totaling $78,000. They earn $100 per month dividends from these stocks. They have no idea of the cost basis for these investments.

Graphic M3 shows the additional assets. Note that the rental is carried at its assessed value.

Prepaying burial expenses still makes sense. Deducting $6,000 for burial costs leaves $123,000 of excess non-exempt resources. What's next?

In looking over their list of non-exempt assets, we calculate first any imbedded costs of liquidation.

$$ Put it in a Box™ Graphic M3

ASSETS — Married Couple, one person in long-term care

RESIDENCE	VEHICLE	TERM LIFE INSURANCE	BURIAL	IRA	PROPERTY RESERVE
Single-family home, no mortgage	Lexus	None	Two plots $6K for pre-burial need	$60K - Dad $200 monthly income $20K - Mom No income	$2,000

Community Spouse Resource Allowance (CSRA)

2004 = $92,760

NON-EXEMPT RESOURCES

Checking and savings accounts	$ 10,000
Certificates of deposit (CDs)	50,000
Additional Vehicles	5,000
Cash value life insurance	4,760
Rental real estate (assessed value)	36,000
Investment accounts	40,000
Any other assests - stocks	78,000
TOTAL	$ 223,760
Property Reserve	(2,000)
Pre-need burial	(6,000)
CSRA (2004 limit)	$ (92,760)
Excess non-exempt resources	$ 123,000

$92,760 ← CSRA (2004 limit)

INCOME

	His	Hers
Social security	$ 1,200	$ 550
Pension	$ 600	
IRA Income	$ 200	
Investment income	$ 200	200
Rental income	$ 300	300
Total	$ 2,500	$ 1,050

Minimum Monthly Maintenance Needs Allowance (MMMNA)
2004 limit = $2,319

Dad and Mom will lose $1,200 of interest if they liquidate their CDs early.

They do not know if their stock portfolio could be sold for a gain or loss and they dread the research necessary to establish cost basis for each stock position.

Selling their rental property would trigger realization of substantial capital gains. Their tax person estimates the capital gains taxes around $15,000.

We want to qualify Dad for benefits without having to incur these costs. Ideally, we want to include all of their non-exempt resources into Mom's Community Spouse Resource Allowance box. Can we do that?

Yes, we can.

We have the option of expanding Mom's CSRA box to include all of the couple's non-exempt resources. This expansion is justified by Mom's low income.

In our previous example, we increased Mom's income to the Minimum Monthly Maintenance Needs Allowance (MMMNA) by allocating income from Dad to Mom. If we choose not to allocate from Dad to Mom (at this stage of application), Mom's income totals $1,050. This is far below the MMMNA of $2,319 (2004 limit). This becomes justification to seek a hearing before an administrative law judge to have Mom's CSRA expanded to include all of their non-exempt resources.

Elder law attorneys have the additional option to increase the CSRA amount through court action. Usually, property transfers from the Ill Spouse to the Well Spouse are included in the court order.

This process requires experienced professional assistance. The initial application for benefits must be denied by the County. An appeal is then filed for a hearing before a state administrative law judge (ALJ). At the hearing, the representative for the applicant presents a brief justifying the CSRA expansion. A County representative will present a brief justifying the County's reasons for denying the original application.

If all goes well, within several weeks the ALJ issues a decision directing the County to include all of the couple's non-exempt resources in an expanded CSRA. Obtaining a CSRA expansion frequently can secure retroactive benefits for up to three months of nursing home costs prior to the month of application.

Graphic M4 illustrates the expansion of the Community Spouse Resource Allowance.

A SPEEDIER ALTERNATIVE

Expanding the CSRA box has drawbacks. Primary is the need for patience as Medi-Cal takes several months to approve a CSRA expansion case.

For some frail, elderly spouses, the prospect of waiting several months for Medi-Cal approval is more than they can handle. Fragile seniors in their 80s and 90s can damage their health by obsessing over the slow Medi-Cal process.

A speedier alternative to CSRA expansion exists through a conversion process that moves assets 'below the line,' i.e., converting non-exempt assets listed in the top half of the *Put it in a Box*™ diagram into monthly income listed at the bottom half of the diagram. We move the assets below the line separating *Assets* and *Income* and create irrevocable income that resembles pension income.

$$ Put it in a Box™ Graphic M4

ASSETS — Married Couple, one person in long-term care

RESIDENCE	VEHICLE	TERM LIFE INSURANCE	BURIAL	IRA	PROPERTY RESERVE
Single-family home, no mortgage	Lexus	None	Two plots $6K for pre-burial need	$60K - Dad $200 monthly income $20K - Mom No income	$2,000

Expanded Community Spouse Resource Allowance (CSRA)

Expanded resource limit encompasses all of couple's non-exempt resources, e.g., $215,760. Spending on pre-need burial not required, but still makes sense.

NON-EXEMPT RESOURCES	
Checking and savings accounts	$ 10,000
Certificates of deposit (CDs)	50,000
Additional Vehicles	5,000
Cash value life insurance	4,760
Rental real estate (assessed value)	36,000
Investment accounts	40,000
Any other assests - stocks	78,000
TOTAL	$ 223,760
Property Reserve	(2,000)
Pre-need burial	(6,000)
CSRA (2004 limit)	$ 215,760

INCOME

	His	Hers
Social security	$ 1,200	$ 550
Pension	$ 600	
IRA Income	$ 200	
Investment income	$ 200	200
Rental income	$ 300	300
Total	$ 2,500	$ 1,050
Maintenance Need	$ (35)	
Allocation	$(1,269) →	1,269
Dad's share of cost	$ 1,196	
Mom's monthly income		$ 2,319

Minimum Monthly Maintenance Needs Allowance (MMMNA)
2004 limit = $2,319

In specific terms, Mom establishes a period-certain immediate annuity that conforms to Medi-Cal specifications. She converts $123,000 of non-exempt resources into irrevocable monthly income that will repay her full investment plus a modicum of interest over a specified period. With the remaining non-exempt resources slotted into the CSRA box, eligibility for Medi-Cal benefits for Dad can be established. Note that the assessed value of the rental can be included in Mom's Community Spouse Resource Allowance, thereby nullifying any need to sell it and incur capital gains taxes. See Graphic M5.

Obtaining eligibility quickly is the advantage to using an immediate annuity. However, with this approach come several significant disadvantages.

To fund the annuity, Mom must liquidate assets that have early withdrawal costs and/or capital gains consequences. Another significant disadvantage concerns Dad's share of cost. Any allocation of income from Dad to Mom is reduced by the amount of income she receives from the annuity. If Mom's income exceeds the MMMNA level, then there is no allocation from Dad to Mom. As shown in Graphic M5, all of his income–less his $35 incidentals allowance–goes to the nursing home for share of cost.

In cases where the Well Spouse has low income, a CSRA expansion is usually the best financial solution for the couple. However, what if the circumstances are reversed and Dad is the Well Spouse and Mom needs nursing home care?

Dad's income of $2,400 exceeds the MMMNA level. This eliminates a CSRA expansion as a viable strategy. Here, using an immediate annuity to convert non-exempt resources to income payable to Dad is the preferred strategy. Dad establishes a short-payout immediate annuity to receive the funds

$$ Put it in a Box™ — Graphic M5

ASSETS — Married Couple, one person in long-term care

Residence	Vehicle	Term Life Insurance	Burial	IRA	Property Reserve
Single-family home, no mortgage	Lexus	None	Two plots $6K for pre-burial need	$60K - Dad $200 monthly income $20K - Mom No income	$2,000

Community Spouse Resource Allowance (CSRA)

2004 = $92,760

NON-EXEMPT RESOURCES

Checking and savings accounts	$ 10,000
Certificates of deposit (CDs)	50,000
Additional Vehicles	5,000
Cash value life insurance	4,760
Rental real estate (assessed value)	36,000
Investment accounts	40,000
Any other assests - stocks	78,000
Total	$ 223,760
Property Reserve (→ Property Reserve)	(2,000)
Pre-need burial (→ Burial)	(6,000)
CSRA (2004 limit) (→ CSRA $92,760)	$ (92,760)
Assets converted to income (→ Annuity Payments)	$ (123,000)
Excess non-exempt resources	$ 0

INCOME

	His	Hers
Social security	$ 1,100	$ 550
Pension	$ 600	
IRA Income	$ 200	
Investment income	$ 200	200
Rental income	$ 300	300
Total	$ 2,400	$ 1,050
Maintenance Need	$ (35)	
Share of Cost	$ 2,365	
Annuity Payments		$ 2,154
Mom's monthly income		$ 3,204

Minimum Monthly Maintenance Needs Allowance (MMMNA) 2004 limit = $2,319

Length of immediate annuity involves many questions: Will Mom receive Dad's pension when he dies? Is she beneficiary of Dad's IRA? Is Dad likely to live for a short or long time? Do we go for fast payback or maximum allocation for as long as Dad lives? Discuss these questions with your advisor.

Estimated payments for 60 mos.

$$ Put it in a Box™ Graphic M6

ASSETS — Married Couple, one person in long-term care

Residence	Vehicle	Term Life Insurance	Burial	IRA	Property Reserve
Single-family home, no mortgage	Lexus	None	Two plots $6K for pre-burial need	$60K - Dad $200 monthly income $20K - Mom No income	$2,000

Community Spouse Resource Allowance (CSRA)

2004 = $92,760

NON-EXEMPT RESOURCES	
Checking and savings accounts	$ 10,000
Certificates of deposit (CDs)	50,000
Additional Vehicles	5,000
Cash value life insurance	4,760
Rental real estate (assessed value)	36,000
Investment accounts	40,000
Any other assests - stocks	78,000
Total	$ 223,760
Property Reserve	(2,000)
Pre-need burial	6,000
CSRA (2004 limit)	$ (92,760)
Assets converted to income	$ (123,000)
Excess non-exempt resources	$ 0

$92,760 ← CSRA (2004 limit)

INCOME	His	Hers
Social security	$ 1,100	$ 550
Pension	$ 600	
IRA Income	$ 200	
Investment income	$ 100	200
Rental income	$ 300	300
Total	$ 2,300	$ 950
Maintenance Need		(35)
Mom's share of Cost		$ 915
Annuity Payments	$ 2,154	
Dad's monthly income	$ 4,454	

Minimum Monthly Maintenance Needs Allowance (MMMNA) 2004 limit = $2,319

Estimated payments for 60 mos.

back as soon as possible. Mom's income will go towards her share of cost. See Graphic M6.

At this point, we need to discuss an important issue that concerns the CSRA limit: How long must a Well Spouse keep his/her assets below the CSRA maximum level? The answer may shock you: **Only for the month of application.**

If Dad is receiving Medi-Cal benefits and Mom lets *her* bank accounts grow to levels above the CSRA limit, will Dad become ineligible? No.

If Dad is receiving benefits and Mom receives an inheritance, does this windfall make Dad ineligible for benefits? No.

If Mom is receiving Medi-Cal benefits and Dad is the Well Spouse: If he converts $123,000 into five years of irrevocable annuity payments of approximately $2,100 per month, will the rapid buildup of his Community Spouse Resource Allowance disqualify Mom for benefits? No.

Snapshot rule: No change in the assets of the Community Spouse will affect the eligibility of the disabled spouse if it happens after the month in which the application is received.

If a Well Spouse wins the California Lottery, will those proceeds disqualify the Ill Spouse for benefits? No, but who would want to keep his/her spouse on Medi-Cal when he or she could pay top dollar for the best private-pay care?

CSRAs AND REDETERMINATIONS

Unfortunately, many Medi-Cal eligibility workers (EWs) and their supervisors are unclear about the one-month-only rule for CSRAs. This confusion becomes evident at redetermination time when EWs tell Well Spouses to spend down their assets to get below the current Community Spouse Resource Allowance limit. If you encounter this problem, get professional assistance. The Medi-Cal consultant or elder law attorney you hire will likely send to the EW and his/her supervisor pages from *All County Welfare Directors Letter No.: 90-01 Questions and Answers Question 12* that addresses this issue, namely:

Once initial eligibility has been established and the CSRA transfer period begins, the county department does not concern itself with the property of the community spouse or the property included in the CSRA.

In some redetermination situations Medi-Cal has a legitimate obligation to request verification of a Well Spouse's assets and income. In cases where a Well Spouse is receiving allocation from an Ill Spouse, EWs are required to verify the Well Spouse's continued eligibility for allocation from the Ill Spouse's income. To accomplish this requirement, EWs must have full disclosure of the Well Spouse's CSRA assets and income. However, EWs should not direct Well Spouses to spend down their *after-acquired CSRA assets.*

USE AND MISUSE OF ANNUITIES

As explained earlier, specialized immediate-pay annuities can be used effectively in some situations to achieve Medi-Cal eligibility and preserve assets for a Well Spouse. Unfortunately, many seniors have been led to purchase 'Medi-Cal qualifying' annuities that in too many instances were not appropriate for their respective financial situations. Here are some guidelines for evaluating annuities for Medi-Cal use.

Usually there is little benefit to consumers to establish an annuity for Medi-Cal purposes beforehand.

(1) If an immediate annuity is the best method to achieve Medi-Cal eligibility, the annuity may be established at the time of need, i.e., in conjunction with filing for benefits. Usually there is little benefit to consumers to establish an annuity for Medi-Cal purposes beforehand.

(2) Annuities must conform to Medi-Cal requirements: a) contract must be irrevocable; b) payment schedule must equal or be shorter than figures listed on Medi-Cal's life expectancy tables; c) must liquidate entirely over proscribed life of annuity. (Life expectancy tables may be found on our website www.savingmomanddad.com.)

(3) Medi-Cal has announced it is actively pursuing authority to recover Medi-Cal payments from annuity payments to beneficiaries.

(4) A Medi-Cal advisor who states he/she processes Medi-Cal applications for free and then places client assets into immediate annuities is not being entirely truthful. The issuing insurance company pays the agent a commission for establishing the immediate annuity. If the agent does not charge fees for processing Medi-Cal applications and relies only on annuity commissions for compensation, a potential conflict of interest exists since annuities are often not the sole, best solution for achieving Medi-Cal eligibility.

(5) On a positive note, immediate annuities allow applicants with non-pension money–also known as non-qualified money–to achieve parity under Medi-Cal

with applicants with significant irrevocable pension income. Thus, the professor with $7,000 of monthly pension does not have an unfair advantage over his twin brother who amassed $700,000 in stocks, bonds and real estate. The entrepreneurial brother may convert his capital into irrevocable annuity income that resembles his brother's academic pension.

(6) Medi-Cal applicants who own deferred annuities can usually annuitize their annuity contracts–convert them to payout or immediate pay status–with the current issuing company. Transferring the deferred annuity to another company's immediate-pay annuity generates a commission for the agent involved but is often unnecessary to meet Medi-Cal requirements.

As we have seen, qualifying for Medi-Cal can be made simple by conforming an applicant's assets and income to fit into Medi-Cal's proscribed categories. However, uneven enforcement of Medi-Cal's rules and regulations result regularly in qualified consumers failing to get benefits.

Though Medi-Cal denial of benefits notices are intimidating, don't accept a denial if you believe you qualify for benefits. Medi-Cal offices usually have contact numbers posted for Legal Aid associations that assist people of limited means. Phone numbers for free legal aid are also listed on the back of *Notice of Action* forms.

Filing an appeal will push a case to the appeals office, where an appeals specialist will examine it. Typically the person filing the appeal of the denial of benefits will receive a mailed notice acknowledging receipt of the appeal filing and provide the appeals specialist name and contact phone number. Contact the appeals specialist and discuss the case. If the appeals specialist agrees that the application was mishandled by the local office, you will be given an opportunity to sign a conditional withdrawal of your appeal, pending re-evaluation by the local office. Procedural errors by a local office are often corrected and benefits approved without going to a hearing before an administrative law judge.

When dealing with Medi-Cal, pay for competent legal and financial assistance if you can afford it. Given the costs of long-term care, paying for professional assistance is usually money well spent.

The preceding case studies encompass 90% of Medi-Cal long-term situations. The next chapter presents additional concepts and facts that, while not used as often, are important to those people who fall into the remaining 10% of Medi-Cal cases.

ALOYSIUS
EARLY 1900S

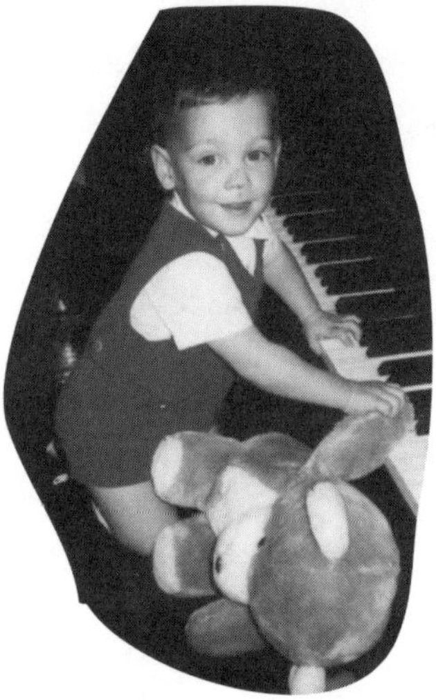

MICHAEL, 1987

CHAPTER 6

ENDS OF THE ECONOMIC SPECTRUM

Automatic eligibility to extreme circumstances

SUPPLEMENTAL SECURITY INCOME (SSI) provides income for elderly, blind and disabled people who have low income and limited financial resources. In general, a person may own a residence and a vehicle, but cannot have more than $2,000 of non-exempt resources. SSI is part of the safety net provided by our federal government to provide a base floor of income for poor people.

SSI recipients must keep their countable non-exempt assets below $2,000 to maintain eligibility.

SSI recipients automatically receive Medi-Cal benefits. Thus, if your Grandmother received SSI while she lived at home, she will automatically qualify for Medi-Cal long-term care benefits if she transfers to a Medi-Cal certified convalescent facility.

The medical coverage that SSI recipients receive from Medi-Cal is often critical to their survival. Receiving an inheritance from a well-meaning relative often provokes a crisis for an SSI recipient, as the disabled person typically will not qualify for private health insurance. Ironically, giving money to a disabled person on SSI could prove detrimental if the gift causes the loss of SSI eligibility.

This crisis can be averted if a Special Needs Trust is established beforehand to receive the inheritance. Ideally, the donating relative will establish the Special Needs Trust as part of his/her estate plan, so the inheritance goes directly into the Special Needs Trust.

The particulars of Special Needs Trusts are too detailed to include in this writing. This is a specialized area of law that requires expert assistance.

The social security website provides information on SSI as well as social security benefits. Go to www.ssa.gov.

MEDI-CAL IN THE COMMUNITY

Like most published information about Medi-Cal, this book focuses on Medi-Cal long-term care benefits. However, Medi-Cal also provides access to health care for poor people who are "in the community." These programs allow a single person to have a house, car and $2,000. A couple is allowed $3,000. Income is also severely restricted for the at-home spouse.

When does Medi-Cal in the community become Medi-Cal long-term care? Confusion reigns among various levels of Medi-Cal concerning long-term care status. Inquiries to county and state officials elicit varied answers.

In one instance where a senior's Medicare benefits had been exhausted, we encountered a situation where local Medi-Cal officials and local hospital officials were adamant that a person who had been receiving acute care in a hospital setting for more than five months could not qualify for Medi-Cal long term status. However, when we appealed the case, the long-term care status was granted. This was important as this status change allowed the at-home spouse to use spousal impoverishment provisions available under Medi-Cal long term programs to protect assets and income.

Medi-Cal is also the payer of last resort when private health insurance benefits are exhausted. Here are case histories of two extreme situations.

Jenny and Jimmie: Jenny, 46, never dreamed she or her husband, Jimmie, 57, would need help paying for medical care. Both worked for large corporations with good health insurance plans. Their income exceeded $160,000 annually. Jimmie's health insurance provided $2 million for major medical expenses. Jenny's plan included $1 million for her spouse.

Jimmie went into the hospital in July for a heart valve replacement. Complications arose. In late November, Jenny came to our office for a consultation. Jimmie was receiving care in a cardio thoracic intensive care unit. The doctors hoped to stabilize him to complete a heart transplant. Jimmie's $2 million of coverage from his health plan plus $1 million of coverage from Jenny's plan had been exhausted during October. Jimmy and Jenny owed over $1 million to the hospital and counting. Jenny had been referred to our office in hopes Jimmie could qualify for Medi-Cal.

Prior to this crisis, Jenny had no reason to know about Medi-Cal. She believed the program assisted low-income people who could not afford health insurance. She also believed that a family could only have a house, car and less than $2,000 of assets to qualify for Medi-Cal assistance.

Jenny and Jimmie's assets included $118,000 in Jimmie's 401k plan, $96,000 in Jenny's 401k plan plus stock options valued at $24,000. They carried a large mortgage on their house and owned three vehicles. Jimmie was receiving $490 per week of state disability income that would stop when $25,480 of benefits had been paid. He was also receiving $4,000 per month of personal disability income payments. Though Jenny earned $80,000 annually, she needed his disability payments to meet their $3,000 monthly mortgage payment.

Eligibility for Medi-Cal long-term care benefits was achieved by verifying the qualified tax status of Jimmie's and Jenny's 401k plans and beginning income withdrawals from Jimmie's 401k plan. Jenny's stock options, their extra two vehicles and their savings in bank accounts totaled less than the allowable community spouse resource allowance (CSRA), so they met Medi-Cal's assets requirements.

However, gaining and continuing eligibility for Jimmie came at a high monthly cost. Because Jenny earned $80,000 from her employment, she was not entitled to any allocation from Jimmie's income. That is, her monthly income exceeded the minimum monthly maintenance allowance (MMMNA), so she did not qualify to receive any allocation of income from Jimmie. All of Jimmie's disability income had to be paid towards his share of cost to maintain eligibility for Medi-Cal benefits.

This posed a significant challenge for Jenny because she depended on their joint incomes to meet their large home mortgage. Withdrawing additional income from Jimmie's IRA would not help her meet her house payments, as such withdrawals would be counted as his income and simply increase his share of cost payments. Withdrawing money from her 401k plan would be very expensive, as such withdrawals would trigger income and penalty taxes that would consume close to fifty percent of each withdrawal.

Jenny had decided to sell their house and move to a smaller, more affordable home when her husband passed away. With $250,000 of life insurance proceeds plus the balance of his 401k plan, Jenny was not forced to sell her home. As a result of Medi-Cal assistance, Jenny was able to maintain her standard of living after her husband exhausted $3 million of private health insurance coverage.

Since the resolution of Jenny and Jimmie's case, several enterprising elder law attorneys have successfully increased income levels for the at-home spouse by obtaining a spousal support order through Family Code Section 4300.

Richard and Martha: For most employees, health insurance provided by their employers is normally sufficient. Richard, 61, and Martha, 60, were both employed and saving for retirement when Martha suffered a major heart attack. In effect, she died. She never regained consciousness. However, paramedics revived her bodily functions.

Martha's health insurance was exhausted after several months paying for hospitalization, intensive care and sub-acute care. Richard was forced to pay $500 per day–$15,000 per month–for sub-acute care to maintain his wife in her comatose state. He had exhausted $200,000 of $600,000 of invested assets and was headed rapidly towards bankruptcy when we assisted him to apply for Medi-Cal benefits.

Richard's and Martha's assets were held in stock accounts with large capital gains tax liabilities. However, since Richard had been paying astronomical sums for Martha's care, the allowable tax deductions for medical costs helped offset capital gains taxes incurred when he liquidated his stock portfolio. Proceeds from the stock sales were used to pay off their home mortgage, with the remainder placed in an immediate annuity to create irrevocable, pension-like income for Richard.

As intended by the originators of the Medicaid spousal impoverishment laws passed in the late 1980s, Richard was not forced into bankruptcy to pay for his wife's care. His wife never regained consciousness. She lived in a vegetative state for five years before she passed away.

The above cases are extreme examples of qualifying for Medi-Cal benefits. The following case example illustrates sophisticated techniques that are used frequently for married couples.

Richard achieved eligibility for Martha despite having joint ownership with his siblings of several vacation properties. His siblings signed affidavits stating their financial reasons for not consenting to the sale of the jointly owned properties. Thus, Richard's financial interests in the properties were unavailable and thereby exempted for Medi-Cal eligibility.

CHAPTER 7

SUE AND HOWARD

Wife's assets and income increased through fair hearings

SUE, 74, WAS CARING FOR HER HUSBAND, Howard, 74, in their home. Howard suffered from Parkinson's and dementia, two progressive diseases that usually lead to confinement in a 24-hour custodial care facility. With that eventuality in mind, Sue sought information about Medi-Cal. She came to her initial consultation burdened by several Medi-Cal myths.

Medi-Cal Myth #1: Sue believed the Well Spouse must always 'spend down' to the current Community Spouse Resource Allowance (CSRA). She believed she would have to decrease their family non-exempt resources to the CSRA limit.

Myth Buster: As explained in earlier chapters, the CSRA may be expanded when a Well Spouse's income is below the Minimum Monthly Maintenance Needs Allowance.

Medi-Cal Myth #2: Sue believed that Medi-Cal would place a recovery lien on their home while Howard was still living.

Myth Buster: Medi-Cal is restricted on placing liens on residences occupied by a Well Spouse when the Ill Spouse dies first. Upon the subsequent death of the Well Spouse, Medi-

Cal may enforce a claim against the Ill Spouse's ownership interest *that existed upon the Ill Spouse's death*. The key is to transfer ownership of the residence to the sole and separate property of the Well Spouse before the Ill Spouse dies. Thus, if the Ill Spouse owns only a single bank account containing less than $2,000 upon his/her death, then Medi-Cal's recovery claim will be limited to the value of that single bank account.

NOTE: Recovery regulations change frequently. Statements about Medi-Cal Recovery in this publication should not be taken as specific legal guidance. Transfers of real estate involve other important considerations, including property tax reassessments, capital gains taxes and designation of sole and separate property interests. Seek appropriate professional assistance to evaluate individual situations.

Medi-Cal Myth #3: Sue believed she would have to liquidate Howard's IRAs, pay the taxes due on the IRA distributions and then place the remainder in her name. She believed this was required because she had been told that Howard could only have $2,000 in his name.

Myth Buster: The Ill Spouse may have only $2,000 of *non-exempt resources* in his/her name. IRAs are exempt resources. Liquidation and re-titling of IRAs is not required to gain or maintain Medi-Cal eligibility. Sue could keep Howard's IRAs intact and simply continue the schedule of required minimum distributions already established for his accounts.

PHYSICAL COSTS OF HOME CARE

As stated earlier, Sue came for her first consultation while her husband was still living at home. She had been cautioned by her physician not to sacrifice her health to provide in-home care for her husband for an extended period. This was wise advice. Most women are not as large or robust as their husbands, which magnifies the challenges they face attempting to lift and transfer their heavier spouses. However, Sue had been married to Howard for 50 years and caring for him at home was something she simply had to do.

Sue returned to our office one year later. Her physical condition had visibly deteriorated. She had developed tendonitis in both shoulders and her weight had dropped from 140 to 126 pounds. Her weakened physical condition plus pressure from her physician and her daughter had convinced her to place Howard in a nursing home.

Her physical condition had visibly deteriorated. She had developed tendonitis in both shoulders and her weight had dropped from 140 to 126 pounds.

Sue's low income justified seeking an expansion of their Community Spouse Resource Allowance to encompass their $135,900 of non-exempt resources. This was accomplished through the appeals process that required four and one-half months to complete. Note: Four to six months is typical for obtaining a CSRA expansion. Similar CSRA expansions can also be effected through 3100 petitions to the probate court.

From their joint monthly family income, Sue was allowed to keep $2,175, the allowable Minimum Monthly Maintenance Needs Allowance (MMMNA) at that time.

Shortly after receiving notice from Medi-Cal of her husband's approval of benefits, Sue suffered a shoulder injury while assisting a nursing home employee to turn her husband in his bed. As a result, Sue was unable to drive, lift her arms above her shoulders or shop for groceries. Before her injury, she cleaned their house and maintained their yard. Her disabilities forced her to pay monthly $70 for a housekeeper and $60 for a gardener.

In situations where the spouse at home incurs unusual medical-related costs, Medi-Cal regulations allow the affected spouse to request a MMMNA increase. An appeal was filed to request an increase of Sue's MMMNA based on her additional monthly outlays for housekeeping and yard work.

The administrative law judge approved the requested changes. However, since her injuries were not permanent, he limited the increase to eight months. Thc ALJ's decision stated that Sue could continue the increased MMMNA past the eight-month period if she could show continued extra costs based on her medical condition.

The administrative law judge approved the requested changes. However, since her injuries were not permanent, he limited the increase to eight months.

At the end of the eight-month period, Sue had recovered from her injuries sufficiently that a continuation of her expanded income allowance was not justifiable. Two months later Howard passed away. As a result of the favorable CSRA and MMMNA rulings, Sue was better able to maintain her finances and home throughout Howard's last days and preserve a decent standard of living for herself after he died.

In general, MMMNA increases are difficult to obtain. Such increases are preponderantly limited to situations where the Well Spouse incurs unusual medical-related expenses. However, as noted earlier, a new method for increasing income levels for Wells Spouses by obtaining spousal support orders through Family Code Section 4300 has been pioneered by some enterprising elder law attorneys.

This chapter described the ordeal of a caregiving wife for her husband. The next chapter addresses the challenges faced by a caregiving daughter who is assisting her mother and father.

Mary, Gramma and Lucy, WWII

David, Pearlie Mae and Delma; Bassfield, Mississippi 1946

Delma, JeNora, Clifton; University of California, San Diego 1993

CHAPTER 8

BARBARA, THE GOOD DAUGHTER

Caring for the Caregiver

"I LOVE MY JOB. I LOVE MY PARENTS. I love my husband." Barbara is a slender woman with long, elegant arms and graceful hands. Barbara is the good daughter, the reliable child who assumes caretaking responsibilities because her two brothers will not. We are seated at a round table with stacks of her parents' papers arrayed before her. She extends her arms and begins touching each pile of paper in rapid succession. "But this is what I feel like I am doing," she says: "I am just so busy trying to do everything."

She confesses that John, her husband, recently vented his frustration. "I have a great husband. He cooks for us, has dinner ready when I come home. But the other day, taking care of my parents got to him." She tells of her husband confronting her "needy" father. "He told my Dad 'You know, the world doesn't revolve around you.' My Dad got all huffy. John was taking him to the doctor. John told my Dad 'I love you, Dad, that's why I'm telling you this. But you only think about yourself. You don't think about how your demands to 'drive you here and there' and 'do this and that' affect other people.'"

Her father was miffed at John. He pouted for several days. Yet the relationship between the two men improved. Barbara observed: "Coming from a non-blood relative, my father was better able to handle it."

Setting boundaries. As aging parents lose capabilities they become more willing to accept assistance from their children. They concede responsibilities because of their diminishing faculties; the children become parents to their parents. Yet the changeover seldom goes smoothly. Dad and Mom request help yet protest the loss of control. Emotions eddy and swirl as responsible children step forward to support parents who vacillate between appreciation and resentment.

With occasional help from her two brothers, Barbara and her husband provide almost daily assistance to her parents. John typically prepares enough food to feed both families. Barbara manages her parents' checking accounts. As evidenced by her solo visit to our office, she seeks professional guidance to assist her aging parents.

She does the work willingly, but her resentment is rising; towards her brothers, her parents, her responsibilities at work. When she views her feelings objectively, she realizes she misses having free time. "We don't fellowship at our church like we used to," she confides: "And I just don't have time to exercise regularly."

Her parents have encouraged her to pay herself out of their funds for the work she does for them. But Barbara is apprehensive about taking any of her parents' money. Occasionally she accepts cash for gas money. However, her desire not to take advantage of her position keeps her from accepting more.

When asked about vacations or get-away weekends for her and John, Barbara laughs wearily and states: "We don't take vacations."

Well, maybe they should take vacations. A system could be established where Dad or Mom writes a check each month for $200 that goes into The Barbara and John Get-Away Weekend Fund. Barbara's eyes light up. "Wow, a weekend away," she says dreamily. Then she confides that $200 per month was the exact amount her parents had suggested paying her.

Bingo. A compromise solution has been identified that minimizes the payment-for-work aspect and maximizes fun-and-gracious-appreciation element. Two hundred dollars per month would not come close to compensating Barbara and John for the assistance they provide. However, such appreciation payments would go a long way towards reducing their resentment and also give her parents opportunity to express their appreciation.

Her intimate exposure to the need for extra income for long-term care services has made Barbara aware of the need to plan for she and her husband. She has begun investigating long-term care insurance, discussed in the next chapter.

SISTERS
LEFT: FLORENCE, GRADUATION 1936
RIGHT: LUELLA, GRADUATION 1939

CHAPTER 9

PEACE OF MIND INSURANCE

How to avoid Medi-Cal and improve long-term care options

OF ALL THE ISSUES WE FACE, the biggest centers on our mortality: When and how will we die? Will we be among the lucky 10% who live life fully and then die suddenly? Or will we be among the 90% who must pass through several stages of diminished capacity before we exit this world?

This issue is so large that many people ignore it. Younger people dismiss notions of mortality. "That's old folks' talk. Don't bother me, I'm too busy living life now." For adults in their 20s, 30s and 40s, the immediacy of careers, marriage and children pushes notions of mortality into the background.

Turning 50, however, changes many things. Mortality becomes more relevant to post-50 individuals as they hear of people their own age succumbing to heart attacks, cancers and other ailments. They see their own physical capabilities diminishing. And they see their once-vibrant parents diminishing before their eyes.

Turning 50, however, changes many things.

Most of us will exit this world in this way: Our quality of health will be stable until a serious medical crisis strikes. Our level of functioning will drop. Normally we will recover, though not to the level we experienced before. This first stage is represented as "1st Crisis" on the following graph.

Upon recovery, we will adjust our lives to fit our lowered level of health. At some point, the 2nd Crisis will occur. Again, our health will drop significantly. We will likely recover, though at a lower level of functioning than before.

Depending on our resilience, these crises will likely continue with our functioning decreasing with each successive crisis. Shortly before we die, a near-fatal crisis will necessitate hospital care followed by skilled nursing care followed by custodial nursing home care.

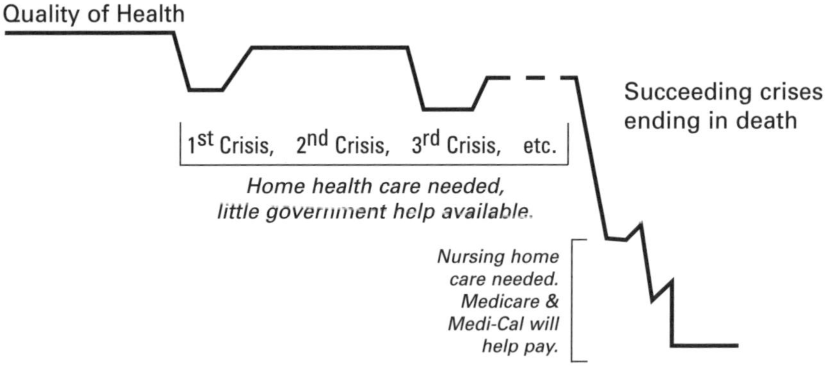

Most discussions about long-term care insurance focus on paying costs of these late-stage crises. However, by the time we–or our parents–enter nursing homes, our bodies as well as our minds will be telling us that the end is near. For the spiritually centered, death is seen as a necessary passage to the afterlife. For many, death is embraced as a welcome release from pain and suffering.

Having financial assistance during your 1st and 2nd Crises is the most important *emotional* reason to have long-term care insurance. At these stages in your life, you will likely retain most of your mental faculties. Maintaining your dignity and control over your care will be important to sustaining your mental and physical health. If you have money to pay for in-home care, you will have better chances of recovering to pre-crisis functioning levels.

From a taxpayer's standpoint, providing financial assistance for less-expensive home health care would make more sense than subsidizing only costly skilled or custodial nursing home care. However, in the topsy-turvy world of American health care, the most expensive levels of care–skilled and custodial–are subsidized. Finding government assistance for less expensive levels of care, such as home health care, is very difficult. The lack of government assistance for in-home health care too frequently leads families to place their elderly members sooner into nursing facilities simply because that is where they can obtain financial assistance.

Activities of Daily Living (ADLs)

- **Bathing**
- **Eating**
- **Dressing**
- **Toileting**
- **Ambulating**
- **Transferring**
- **Continence**

Functional impairment caused by dementia and Alzheimer's disease will also trigger benefits.

ACCESSING BENEFITS

Question: If what we want most is assistance to pay for home health care, what physical circumstances must exist for in-home health care benefits to be paid from a long-term care policy?

Answer: An insured person must be unable to perform two of seven activities of daily living (ADLs) to qualify for any benefits from a long-term care policy.

Qualifying for two ADLs means you must be seriously ill. It is possible that your 1st Crisis will not impinge your health sufficiently for you to qualify for home health care benefits and you will need to draw on personal assets to cover in-home health care costs.

Another issue involves the waiting period–also known as the elimination period–that must be met before a policy will start paying benefits. When shopping for coverage, look for policies that allow insureds to accumulate waiting days. For example, during your 1st Crisis you met the two-out-of-seven ADL requirement for 20 of the 60 days in your policy's elimination period. When you meet the ADL requirement for an additional 40 days during your 2nd Crisis, your policy will now begin paying benefits.

In recognition of consumers' desire for more accessible in-home health care, some LTC insurance carriers now offer comprehensive policies with traditional 30-, 60-, and 90-day elimination periods for nursing home care and zero elimination days for in-home health care benefits. Such policies provide in-home benefits as soon as you meet the two-out-of-seven ADL requirement.

WHEN TO BUY?

When should you consider purchasing LTC insurance? 'While you are still healthy' is a flippant yet accurate answer. None of us knows what lies around the next corner of our lives. We steadfastly hope and pray that we remain healthy, yet debilitating illnesses afflict people at many ages.

Generally, LTC insurance experts recommend that people who pass their 50th birthday should consider purchasing some form of peace-of-mind coverage. Our propensity to contract or develop debilitating afflictions increases significantly once we pass our 50th milestone.

AUTOMOBILE VERSUS LIFE INSURANCE

LTC insurance polices are typically grouped as either traditional LTC or life insurance LTC.

Traditional LTC is similar to automobile insurance: You pay premiums and hope you never use the coverage. If you 'Get Lucky' and drop dead, usually your heirs will receive no residual benefits for the premiums that were paid; 'usually' because you can put refund provisions on traditional LTC, however, such provisions increase premiums significantly. Note: One carrier offers interesting residual benefits to couples. If each person pays premiums for LTC coverage for ten years and then one person dies without using any policy benefits, the surviving spouse's policy becomes completely paid up.

By contrast, life insurance LTC will pay your heirs life insurance death benefits if you die without using LTC benefits or use only a small portion of your benefits. If you need LTC benefits, the life insurance policy pre-pays the death benefit. Normally these policies provide four years of LTC benefits, with the first two years of benefit coming from the original policy and the final two years paid from an LTC rider. Note: Once you have used the LTC benefits for two years, your heirs will receive only minor residual life insurance benefits.

Within these two general descriptions of long-term care insurance are many variations. LTC is a relatively new field, having come to public attention over the last twenty years. Here are some general points to consider about LTC insurance:

Choose an established company with good safety and credit ratings. You want an insurance company that is profitable so it is around to pay your benefits.

Shy from companies with unusually low premiums. Again, you want your carrier to operate profitably. If a company's premiums are significantly lower than its competitors, you have to wonder how long that firm will remain financially solvent.

Evaluate whether California Partnership long-term care policies are suitable for your situation. Partnership policies pay benefits in the same ways other traditional long-term care policies with an additional benefit: Each dollar a Partnership policy pays for your long-term care benefits allows you to keep an extra dollar of non-exempt resources should you apply for Medi-Cal benefits. You can learn more about Partnership policies on the Internet. Type in 'California partnership for long-term care' into the 'Search' function of your browser and numerous helpful sites will appear.

Pay an independent advisor an hourly or flat fee to analyze your financial and health considerations and present two to three alternatives for you.

Everyone's situation is unique, yet similar to others. Herewith are examples of policies that consumers chose to meet their individual needs. *All names have been changed to protect confidentiality.*

DECEMBER-MAY MARRIAGE

Jordan and Gracie have a December-May marriage. Eighteen years older than Gracie and the primary breadwinner, Jordan, age 69, wanted to protect their substantial asset base for Gracie in the likely event he predeceases her. At the time the policy was established in 1995, their net worth exceeded $1.2 million. Jordan earned about $5,000 monthly from ongoing business efforts. Gracie had recently become disabled.

In many published articles about LTC insurance, financial journalists tend to identify $1 million of net worth as the level where most couples will self-insure their potential LTC liabilities. However, in discussions with veteran LTC insurance agents and brokers, many wealthy and affluent people above the $1 million net worth level purchase LTC insurance so their spouses and/or beneficiaries will not have to tap family assets for end-of-life costs.

Jordan's loss upon surrender would be limited to the potential interest or other gains he may have made investing the money elsewhere.

Jordan placed $61,886 into a single-premium whole life insurance policy with LTC benefits. This premium purchased $86,100 of immediate life insurance coverage. Jordan's high blood pressure plus other minor heart concerns increased the amount of premium necessary to buy this level of insurance coverage for a man age 69.

If Jordan dies suddenly without accessing any LTC benefits from this policy, Gracie will receive life insurance proceeds of $86,100. If Jordan becomes ill and can not perform two out of seven ADLs for 90 days, this policy will pay $117 per day for nursing home and/or home health care benefits over a maximum benefit period of four years.

Jordan views this coverage as insurance to protect their asset base for Gracie. However, since none of us knows who will leave this earth first, what happens if Gracie dies before Jordan? Jordan can choose to keep the policy for his heirs or turn it in to receive its current cash value. Interestingly, if Jordan decides to turn in this policy before drawing any LTC benefits, he is guaranteed to receive back at least the full amount of his initial premium, $61,886.

This is unusual, as most life insurance policies carry surrender fees that can be significant, especially if a policy is returned within a few years of its issue. Jordan's loss upon surrender would be limited to the potential interest or other gains he may have made investing the money elsewhere. After the policy has been in force for several years, the cash value would begin to build and its surrender value would rise accordingly.

STEVEN AND NANCY

Steven and Nancy adopted a baby when they were both in their early 40s. By the time their son, Aaron, was 10 years old, Steven and Nancy had both observed their 50th birthdays and were beginning to think about their long-term care provisions. Steven stated their desire clearly: "We don't want to be a burden to our son when he's in his 20s and 30s building his career and family." When Nancy began showing signs of unusual fatigue and persistent low-grade pain that her doctors could not readily identify nor cure, Steven and Nancy decided to seek LTC coverage.

Due to her fatigue problems, several LTC carriers wanted significantly higher premiums to insure Nancy or declined to offer coverage altogether. Since Steven also wanted coverage, they viewed their potential LTC costs as a single, joint monthly payment. Eventually they found what they wanted: A monthly-pay, second-to-die whole life insurance policy with death benefit of $150,000 and LTC benefits. (Second-to-die means that two lives are insured, however the death benefit is not paid until the second insured dies.)

Nancy believes she will eventually need daily assistance at home to bathe and dress.

Steven and Nancy bought their policy with a three percent simple inflation benefit increase rider and a lifetime benefits rider. The initial LTC benefit for each person was $3,000 per month for home health care or nursing home coverage, beginning after the ill person has met the two-out-of-seven-ADLs requirement for 90 days.

Due to the joint life coverage, Nancy's condition and the two riders, the premiums for this policy equal $336.23 per month or $4,034.76 per year. Before committing to the policy in 1996, Steven and Nancy pondered if they should instead invest the monthly premium into a growth investment that could pay towards their long-term care. However, several years after they obtained the coverage, Nancy's conditioned worsened to the point she had to stop working. Nancy believes she will eventually need daily assistance at home to bathe and dress. Given the volatile performance of stock market growth investments during recent years, Steven and Nancy are glad they choose instead to invest their monthly payments into long-term care insurance. They are relieved that their LTC policy will provide money to pay for long-term care whenever it becomes necessary.

JOHN AND MARY

John, 67, and Mary, 56, retired from their respective careers in 2002. Their social security and pension benefits are similar. Each is relatively healthy. They looked forward to buying a vacation home away from Los Angeles and traveling the country in their truck and fifth-wheel travel trailer. Their retirement assets and income will afford them comfortable though not lavish lifestyles.

Since their financial resources are similar and each wants to protect assets for the other, John and Mary sought LTC coverage from an established carrier with "reasonable" premiums. With their good health histories and lack of bad habits–smoking, excessive eating or drinking alcohol–John and Mary qualified for preferred premiums.

Traditional LTC insurance is purchased as a daily benefit for a set number of years of benefit. For healthy people with moderate incomes and assets, what level of LTC coverage is sensible?

Statistics concerning the usage of and need for LTC insurance vary, but industry participants agree generally on these points:

- At age 65, a woman has a one-in-two chance of spending some time in a nursing home.
- At age 65, a man has a one-in-three chance of spending some time in a nursing home.
- The majority of nursing home patients stay less than three months. Either they get better and go home or they do not get better and they go to heaven. A 1999 study conducted by the National Center for Health Statistics compiled these length-of-stay statistics for men and women ages 75-84:

Length of stay	Men (%)	Women (%)
Less than 1 month	43	38
1-3 months	20	19
3-6 months	10	8
6-12 months	7	9
1-2 years	9	7
2-3 years	4	5
3-5 years	4	6
6-10 years	3	6
10+ years	0	2

No one knows the optimum level of LTC insurance for anyone because no one knows the future. People must balance their desires for peace of mind versus their perception of the risks of no coverage. Often this discussion becomes more of an emotional than rational decision due to the tradeoffs involved: What current pleasures must be given up to buy peace of mind with long-term care insurance?

Peace of mind		Perceived risks of no coverage
Cost of LTC insurance	vs.	Less discretionary 'fun' money

▲

John and Mary studied the issues and purchased individual LTC policies that pay $110 per day for three years of home health care and/or nursing home care after meeting a 90-day elimination period. Each policy includes a five percent compound inflation rider so benefits will increase as time passes. For these coverages, they pay $1,200.94 annually for John's coverage and $853.38 annually for Mary's coverage, or $2,054.32 total annual premiums. Neither policy carries residual benefits.

MERCEDES

A single woman, Mercedes, 71 years old in 1996, lived comfortably in an inherited two-bedroom condominium in an upscale senior living community. She received monthly income of $1,400 and her invested assets totaled $268,000. Mercedes lacked close family support and worried about the quality of care she might receive during her last years.

Due to her limited income, Mercedes could not afford to pay monthly premiums for traditional LTC insurance. However, she had $90,000 invested in low-yielding certificates of deposit. Interest earned from these CDs was being reinvested.

Mercedes chose to move $43,444.29 from matured CD accounts into a single premium life insurance policy with LTC benefits. This single premium purchased in July 1996 provided $73,000 of life insurance and $146,000 of long-term care benefits. The policy will pay $100 per day nursing home and/or home health care benefits after Mercedes satisfies a 90-day waiting period. If Mercedes does not take any withdrawals for approximately nine years, the policy should have earned enough interest to increase the cash value and also increase the daily benefit amounts.

Her invested funds would earn interest at rates established by the issuing company that could not go lower than the policy's guaranteed four percent crediting rate. Mercedes could receive back her initial premium at any time with no early withdrawal penalties.

RISING AWARENESS OF LTC AVAILABILITY

Long-term care insurance has risen to the level of national awareness. Insurance companies are jockeying for brand name recognition as baby boomers evaluate the costs and benefits of long-term care insurance. Large corporations are beginning to offer long-term care insurance as an employee benefit. The federal government recently added long-term care insurance as an optional benefit for their employees.

California state employees may purchase long-term care insurance through the Public Employees Retirement System (PERS). Public school educators may buy LTC insurance through the State Teachers Retirement System (STRS).

Reams of information about LTC insurance are available on the Internet. Entering "long term care insurance needs assessment" on a popular search engine yields multiple pages of website listings. Links to informative LTC web pages are contained on www.savingmomanddad.com.

Paying a consultation fee to an experienced long-term care insurance advisor to analyze your situation and develop specific recommendations will likely be money well spent. Paying a fee for advice will most likely result in a more objective evaluation.

Paying fees for expert legal guidance, discussed in the next chapter, is also prudent planning.

CAROLE

STEVE, JO ANN, SUSAN, JOE, CORA, MARGARET
1982

CHAPTER 10

LEGAL STUFF OVERSIMPLIFIED

Legal questions everyone needs answered

MOM HAS FOUR GROWN CHILDREN: Richard, Robert, Roger and Raymond. She loves them equally. When her husband was living, she and her husband owned their assets as joint tenants with rights of survivorship. This widely used form of ownership ensures easy transfer of property to the surviving joint tenant.

When Dad died five years ago, Mom became sole owner of their assets. At that time, Mom's tax person advised her to see an attorney to set up a will and possibly a trust. Mom told her tax person (and herself) she would call an attorney soon. In the meantime, she handwrote a will leaving her assets equally to her four sons. However, to avoid forcing her sons to process her will through probate, she added her eldest son, Richard, as a joint tenant to all of her assets.

Q. What happens to Mom's assets (and relations among her four sons) if she dies without correcting her estate plan?

A. Upon Mom's death, all of her assets go to Richard, the surviving joint tenant. Though her handwritten will is likely valid in California, it serves little legal purpose because her assets went to Richard as the surviving joint tenant. Understandably, relations among the four brothers will sour, despite Richard's protestations to his brothers about his ignorance of Mom's estate plan.

Q. Suppose Richard wants to restore good relations with his brothers. What are potential negative tax consequences to Richard and his brothers as he divides his newly inherited assets among his brothers?

A. Depending on factors involved, Richard and his brothers may incur capital gains taxes upon sale of their mother's capital assets, i.e., her home and stock portfolio. Additionally, depending on the size of Richard's estate and the current estate and gift tax exemptions, he may suffer negative estate tax consequences as he distributes Mom's assets among his brothers. If he is lucky, he will find a tax advisor and/or attorney who can show Richard how to solve these challenges. All in all, it's a mess because Mom was too lazy and/or cheap to hire an attorney.

Richard may possibly be treated as a constructive trustee for his siblings. That way he is a conduit and not a donor, so there is no gift tax upon redistribution. Seek professional assistance for such situations.

Moral of the story: Get competent professional help when dealing with legal and financial matters. Any reasonably-competent tax person, attorney, financial advisor or banker would have alerted Mom to the folly of her planning if she had simply asked for guidance.

To get your affairs in order, address these issues:

- If I become unable to make legal and financial decisions for myself, whom would I trust to make those decisions for me? How can I give that person legal authority to act for me when I become incapacitated?

- What level(s) of medical care do I want when I become seriously ill? Do I want my doctors to use every medical option available to keep me breathing for as long as possible? Should they make 'heroic efforts' to keep me going?
- How will I pay for long-term care? If I am forced to accept custodial care in a nursing home, do I want all of my assets used to pay for my care? Do I want to utilize Medi-Cal planning strategies to preserve assets for my beneficiaries?
- What burial arrangements do I want?
- Whom do I trust to distribute my assets according to directions in my will and/or trust? Do I want one of my children to handle these unpopular responsibilities or would I prefer a corporate trustee?

When you address these issues squarely, the benefit of seeking professional legal guidance should become apparent to you. If you have professional relations with a tax person or financial advisor, ask for referrals to established estate planning attorneys.

Seeking competent professional help is a theme running through this book. The next chapter provides assistance to select advisors to advise you on Medi-Cal and other long-term care options.

Paul and Mary Jane; November 24, 1947

CHAPTER 11

CHOOSING A MEDI-CAL ADVISOR

Questions to ask prospective Medi-Cal advisors

FIRST ASK YOURSELF: Am I typically penny-wise and pound-foolish? This is an important consideration when seeking a competent elder finance or elder law advisor.

If you answer 'Yes' to the above question, then you will likely be satisfied working with advisors who charge lower fees and deliver limited services. For example, former Medi-Cal eligibility workers advertise their services as Medi-Cal advisors. While these advisors understand Medi-Cal's rules and regulations, they are often unschooled about financial planning, investing and legal matters. If you are content to pay for Medi-Cal-only guidance, such advisors may fulfill your needs. They typically charge less than professionally credentialed financial advisors and elder law attorneys.

Another avenue for penny-wise, pound-foolish consumers is to secure assistance from advisors who claim to charge *nothing* to assist you with your Medi-Cal application. This actually comes under the heading of TINSTAAFL: **There Is No Such Thing As A Free Lunch**. When queried how they are paid for their services, these advisors answer with some variation on this theme: "The companies I work for pay me." Translated into plain English, this means they receive commissions for re-routing your assets into different investments.

Medi-Cal qualifying annuities are typically the investment vehicle of choice. *Caveat emptor:* Let the buyer beware.

If you prefer to use professionally-credentialed advisors who tell you upfront their services and fees and who know how financial planning, investing and legal matters integrate with Medi-Cal, then the following list of questions will prove helpful to finding and selecting a competent advisor. These questions are designed for consumers who know little or nothing about Medi-Cal or Medi-Cal advisors.

Q. How can a family increase the amount of assets a spouse at home can keep?

A. Best answer: The advisor will talk about increasing the Community Spouse Resource Allowance through a fair hearing or court petition. Whatever is said, go to the next question.

Unacceptable answer: "There is no way to increase the amount of assets a spouse can keep."

Q. Can you provide names and contact numbers for two clients that you have represented at fair hearings or in court?

A. Best answer: "Yes, I can. However, I must first check with them before I give you their phone numbers."

Unattractive answer: "I've never had to go to a hearing. I make sure my cases are right before I submit them." (Likely indicates an advisor with limited Medi-Cal experience.)

Unacceptable answer: "I don't give out my clients' names and numbers."

If the advisor is unwilling to provide references, go to the next advisor on your list. If the advisor provides references, call them. You know the advisor will only provide names of satisfied clients, but call them anyway. Talking with the advisor's clients will give you a feel for his/her manner of conducting business.

Q. How do clients pay for your services?

A. Best answer: "I charge hourly or flat fees for consultations and processing Medi-Cal applications from A to Z."

Expensive answer: "I charge a fee based on a percentage of my client's assets."

Unacceptable answer: "I handle Medi-Cal cases for free."

Q. For non-attorney advisors: What professional designations do you hold?

A. Best answers (any one or more): CFP-Certified Financial Planner, ChFC-Chartered Financial Consultant, CLU-Chartered Life Underwriter, CPA-Certified Public Accountant, EA-Enrolled Agent. May also encounter qualified advisors with medical or other designations, such as RN–Registered Nurse or Forensic Examiner–Consultant. Less attractive answers: Little-known designations containing words 'senior' or 'elderly.'

Q. For financial advisors: How do you handle wills and trusts and power of attorneys?

A. Best answer: "I am very familiar with estate planning documents and know how they work with Medi-Cal, however, I do not draft such documents. I am not licensed to practice law. If you have a relationship with an established estate planning attorney, I will coordinate our efforts with your attorney. If you do not have an established relationship with an estate planning attorney, we will provide names of two to three established estate planning attorneys that we have worked with over the years."

B. Highly unattractive answer: "I am not an attorney but

I work with an attorney in _____" (names a faraway city) "who reviews all my work. I can help you draft your estate planning documents for much lower fees than those charged by local attorneys."

You have worked all of your life to accumulate your resources. However large or small that amount is, you earned it and you want to direct its use. Trying to save a few dollars on estate planning fees is clearly penny-wise and pound-foolish. When you need estate planning help, get experienced help from an experienced estate planning attorney.

Q. For elder law attorneys: Do you handle our financial matters in connection with our application for Medi-Cal?

A. Best answer: "I understand how financial assets and income work with Medi-Cal but I am not a financial advisor. If you have a financial advisor who is willing to follow our directions explicitly, then we will coordinate our work with your advisor. If you don't have an established relationship with a financial advisor, we will provide names of two or three advisors that we have worked with over the years."

B. Unattractive answer: "Yes, we handle everything for you."

You have worked all of your life to accumulate your resources. However large or small that amount is, you earned it and you want to direct its use. Having elder law/estate planning attorneys direct your investing makes no more sense than having financial advisors draft your legal documents. You want a team approach where each professional keeps your needs uppermost. You do not want individual egos to get in the way of your best interests.

Follow the '3 Cs' for evaluating advisors: Competence, compassion, cooperation. You want advisors who know what they know, embody compassion for individuals in crisis and cooperate with other advisors to seek the best solutions for your individual situation.

Q. For all advisors: What percentage of your business comes from elder finance or elder law work?

A. Best answer: Twenty-five percent or more.

B. Unattractive answer: Ten percent or less.

Q. For all advisors: How long have you been working directly with Medi-Cal cases?

A. Best answer: Three or more years

B. Unattractive answer: Less than three years

Competent advisors usually charge a flat fee for an initial consultation, with fees typically ranging from $250 to $500. Given the high costs of nursing home care, paying for two separate consultations may be a good investment.

When you go for an initial consultation, bring *everything*: bank statements, investment account statements, wills, trusts, powers of attorney, insurance polices and statements, burial arrangements, real estate trust deeds, notices from hospitals and nursing homes, papers for any earlier applications. If you or your relative is not organized, overcome your embarrassment and bring along the boxes and files full of miscellaneous *stuff*. Good advisors want to hear from you about Mom's situation but they need to see current documents to verify her financial and legal condition.

If you pay for professional guidance, follow your advisor's instructions explicitly. As explained previously, Medi-Cal and other affiliated aid programs follow regulations that often do not make sense to consumers. You hire an advisor because that person knows *bureaucratese*, which is a foreign language to inexperienced consumers. Do you and your loved ones a huge favor and don't second-guess your advisor. If you are skeptical about your advisor's directions, say so. If you really question your advisor's directions, seek a second opinion.

Good advisors know how to interface with Medi-Cal. They know the wisdom of treating Medi-Cal employees with respect and courtesy, as discussed in the next chapter.

FRANKIE, 1954

CHAPTER 12

ELIGIBILITY WORKERS HAVE FEELINGS, TOO

Treat Medi-Cal workers as people, not bureaucrats

LET ME RECOUNT A CASE I handled with a colleague over ten years ago.

Mom had an aged Cadillac that was gasping for life. Mom needed to be transported regularly to her doctor. Daughter's car was small, aged and unreliable, so upgrading Mom's car made sense. However, I advised Daughter to stay away from luxury names. "Forget Cadillac, Lincoln, Lexus, Infinity. Yes, a luxury car meets Medi-Cal regulations but think how that may be perceived by the Medi-Cal staff," I counseled her.

She ignored my admonitions. She purchased a near-new Cadillac.

I can't prove anything since I have no access to the daily inner workings of any Medi-Cal office. Neither does my colleague. But I can tell you this: Medi-Cal nit-picked that case six ways to Sunday. A relatively simple case turned ugly. My colleague finally achieved eligibility for Mom after months of tedious back-and-forth communication with the local Medi-Cal office.

Neither my colleague nor I have any proof that purchasing the Cadillac caused the case to go sour. But we believe that Daughter's arrogant behavior pushed someone's button. And frankly, I couldn't really fault the Medi-Cal workers if they sidetracked the case.

Consider the plight of the Medi-Cal eligibility worker (EW). Medicaid laws are written in Washington, passed to states for oversight and to counties for administration. Medicaid becomes Medi-Cal in California. Medi-Cal has worked with draft regulations since the rules changeover January 1, 1990, which means the current regulations used by all Medi-Cal offices throughout California have never formally been implemented! No wonder confusion reigns.

Consider the plight of the Medi-Cal eligibility worker

After 14 years helping individuals and families apply for Medi-Cal assistance, I can testify to these truths about Medi-Cal eligibility workers: They are overworked, underpaid and undertrained. They do not write regulations. However, they are charged with enforcing them and doing so with minimal, uneven training. On a daily basis EWs must confront frustrated consumers who don't know the maddening complexity of multiple assistance programs offered through the Department of Social Services. And, as in the case of my Cadillac-buying client, they daily see people who deliberately abuse the system with outrageous behavior.

You can help your application move faster through the system by viewing your case from the EW's perspective. An EW must verify your right to financial assistance; the EW's job depends on it. So make the EW's life easier. Provide copies of all verifications promptly. Don't ask "Why do I have to provide this?" instead ask "Can you tell me the best way to get the verifications you need?" Many offices allow applicants to mail in applications. Provide *everything* on the list. If you don't have a requested verification, include a business-like typed cover letter stating you are making efforts to secure the item.

Never raise your voice to an eligibility worker or supervisor. Always speak courteously. Angry demands only get you sidelined as a possible nut case.

You cannot judge EWs by their outward appearance. Several years ago I met with two workers in individual meetings in the same office during the same week. The first meeting was held with Ms. Prim-n-Proper. Her hair looked nice, she dressed professionally and appeared well organized. My second meeting was with Ms. I-Need-a-Makeover. Her brown shirt fit poorly, her hair badly needed attention and she did not seem well organized.

Ms. Prim-n-Proper turned out to be a royal pain in the neck. Pompous and inflated with self-importance, she sent nit-picking requests for insignificant information and played haughty whenever I called to discuss the case. I finally took the unusual action of calling her unit manager to get my client's case handled fairly.

Ms. I-Need-a-Makeover may not have paid much attention to her looks but she certainly paid attention to her work. Her attitude was simple: Let's get the job done. If your client qualifies, let's prove it and get on with it. If your client does not qualify, I'm going to tell you why in plain English. I don't have time for stroking your ego or mine. If I need verifications, I'm going to pick up the phone and tell you what I need. Not surprisingly, the case she handled was approved much faster than the case handled by her office mate.

Sometimes you may find a worker who is willing to take personal risks to assist consumers. For several years I regularly received calls from clients who had been referred to me by an eligibility worker who had heard me speak at a conference. He could not advise individuals directly about their finances but he would discreetly recommend that they call me to discuss their applications for benefits. He did this because he believed that uninformed consumers should receive similar benefits as consumers who had professional representation.

I encountered recently in one Medi-Cal office unfamiliarity about a benefit program that was used routinely by neighboring offices. Known by the name of the lawsuit that originated the benefit, *Hunt vs. Kizer* allows Medi-Cal recipients to use old, unpaid medical bills to offset monthly share-of-cost payments. This can be useful to free up money to pay off unpaid medical bills with share-of-cost money that otherwise would go to the state. The occasion to use *Hunt vs. Kizer* arose recently for an elderly man who was being hounded by debt collectors for ambulance and assorted medical bills his wife had incurred before she qualified for Medi-Cal benefits.

***Hunt vs. Kizer* allows Medi-Cal recipients to use old, unpaid medical bills to offset monthly share-of-cost payments.**

The Medi-Cal office in question should have known how to handle *Hunt vs. Kizer* requests. However, operating under the maxim 'Honey catches more flies than vinegar,' I devised a low-key strategy to educate local Medi-Cal officials and obtain favorable results for the elderly man.

First, I politely requested from my client's eligibility worker instructions on applying old, unpaid medical bills to share of cost under *Hunt vs. Kizer*. The eligibility worker expressed his ignorance of the program and said he would investigate.

When I had not heard back from him after one week, I called. He reported that his supervisors were also not familiar with the program but were researching it. I mentioned that I had found information that might help their research. I offered to forward the material to him. He accepted my offer. I downloaded from www.dhs.ca.gov All County Welfare Directors Letter 93-63 and delivered it to the Medi-Cal office.

This ACWD letter contains more than 50 pages. That means I downloaded 50 pages from a government website, printed them and gave to government employees who should have known about the program in the first place or certainly where to find updated information. In a perfect world, I would not have to do that. However, we live imperfectly in an imperfect world, so I discreetly supplied the information.

Within three weeks, my client's *Hunt vs. Kizer* request was processed. My client used the extra money to pay off the bills and end the threatening contacts from the collection agencies.

I share this story both to raise awareness of the *Hunt vs. Kizer* program and recommend the benefits of remaining considerate and level headed when seeking benefits from Medi-Cal. At professional conferences and networking meetings, I frequently hear of difficult cases where I believe cooperation rather than confrontation might have yielded better results. Though the Medi-Cal advisor might tell the story to highlight the incompetence and intransigence of Medi-Cal officials, too often I hear in the telling a penchant for confrontation that blinds the advisor to low-key, cooperative resolutions.

Whether working with Medi-Cal or other governmental organizations, remember that the person handling your requests has feelings, too. Treat them courteously and respectfully and you are more likely to receive similar treatment in return.

With dramatic changes pending in the way penalties for transfers of assets are calculated, consumers and advisors are advised to keep pace with changes in Medi-Cal regulations. Buyers of this book who provide an email address will receive periodic notifications of major changes in Medi-Cal rules and regulations from the author.

A description of the current method for handling transfers is discussed in the next chapter.

CHAPTER 13

LEGITIMATE TRANSFERS

Rules and sanctions for gifting assets and applying for benefits

MEDI-CAL MYTH: Medi-Cal looks back three years for gifts. Gifts of any size will disqualify an applicant for benefits.

Myth Buster: Medi-Cal may look back for gifts 30 months, 36 months or 60 months, depending on various circumstances. However, what is more important is how Medi-Cal assesses periods of ineligibility, i.e., penalty periods, for giving assets away and then applying for benefits.

Example: During December your grandmother gifted $10,000 to you and $10,000 to your spouse. Now it's February, Grandmother resides in a Medi-Cal certified nursing home and you want to apply for Medi-Cal benefits for her. How will Medi-Cal treat these gifts?

Each year the Department of Health Services announces the average private pay rate (APPR) in an All County Welfare Directors Letter that is typically issued during February. For 2004, the APPR is $4,477 (The 2005 APPR will be listed on www.savingmomanddad.com and sent as an email to book buyers who provide an email address). This number represents the average cost of one month's custodial care in a nursing home in California. Eligibility workers use this number to calculate whether gifts impact an applicant's eligibility for Medi-Cal benefits.

In grandmother's case, the amount of the gifts is totaled and divided by the APPR to determine the number of months of ineligibility. The penalty period begins with the month the gift was made. So we calculate: $20,000 divided by $4,477 equals 4.47 months. This number is rounded *down* to four months. Starting with December we count three additional months–January, February, March–to determine that by April Grandmother may apply for Medi-Cal long-term care benefits and not have her eligibility affected by two $10,000 gifts made in December.

This is the standard, conservative method for calculating gifting penalties. At the time of this writing, a controversial method called 'stacked gifting' has been practiced by aggressive Medi-Cal consultants and elder law attorneys. In stacked gifting, a penalty period is calculated for each gift and the penalty periods run concurrently. Thus, $10,000 divided by $4,477 equals 2.23 months, which is rounded down to two months. If penalties for Grandmother's two $10,000 gifts are run concurrently, then she is ineligible for only two months, or half the time if the penalties are run consecutively. Other stacked gifting techniques involve making consecutive transfers on different days to the same recipients.

Legislation passed in 1993 but not fully implemented in California rules out stacked gifting. This inaction at the State level allows aggressive Medi-Cal consultants and elder law attorneys to exploit a legal loophole that allows extravagant transfers by individuals who then qualify for Medi-Cal benefits. However, Medi-Cal officials at state levels indicate that stacked gifting will soon be outlawed. (Regulations outlawing stacked gifting are expected during 2004.)

All gifting comes with attendant dangers. Potential heirs who favor gifting should know that government agencies look for cases of elder fiduciary abuse. This is where someone–usually a younger family member–uses coercion or undue influence to convince an elderly person to give away his or her assets. Authorities especially look for fiduciary abuse when a power of attorney has been used to transfer funds away from an elderly person.

Each person must decide for him/herself the ethics of gifting. In general, I advise seniors to not gift assets to their offspring. To give away their assets is to turn over control of their lives to their adult children. However, seniors too often feel they must make gifts to keep the allegiance of their offspring.

Seniors too often feel they must make gifts to keep the allegiance of their offspring.

Not surprisingly, potential heirs are more interested in gifting than seniors. Adult offspring typically say 'We want what's best for Mom,' yet their eyes glow when the subject of gifting arises. I have angered potential heirs during family consultations when I have cautioned parents about giving money to their offspring.

In one instance, Son-in-law and Daughter would interrupt whenever I spoke directly to Mom. Finally I tactfully yet directly told Son-in-law and Daughter that I needed to talk to Mom without interruption. Son-in-law accepted my statement, but Daughter folded her arms, stuck out her lower lip and said belligerently: "Are you telling me to shut up?!"

"I need to talk to your mother without being interrupted," I replied in my most professional, even-handed voice. I proceeded to discuss with Mom how gifting her assets and home to her children would turn over to them control of her life. Mom smiled throughout our discussion while Daughter sat back in her chair and sulked.

FRIENDLY CON GAME

During the 1990s I served on a task force that brought together law enforcement, health care agencies, social workers, bankers, elder law attorneys and other parties to combat elder fiduciary abuse.

In one case a younger couple befriended an elderly man who lived in a mobile home park. The younger man worked as a groundskeeper and fix-it-man for the complex. His wife became friendly with the elderly man. Soon he was giving the couple money.

A concerned social worker contacted the task force. This case had the hallmarks of a well-known con game where itinerant criminals befriend elderly people as a prelude to emptying their bank accounts.

Law enforcement officials investigated the situation but were stopped short when the elderly man expressed support of the helpful young couple. He said they paid attention to him while his family did not. The elderly man appeared to be of sound mind, so petitioning a court to appoint a conservator was ruled out. Other than warning the young couple that they were being scrutinized, there was little else to do. Law enforcement can't stop a competent person from giving away his or her assets.

Sadly, Mom was emotionally dependent on Daughter. Daughter had moved Mom to Southern California from Northern California where Mom had lived for many years. This left Mom with no established network of friends and church acquaintances. She was forced to depend on family members who seemed as interested in her assets as they were her health care. Unfortunately, these circumstances are too familiar to people who strive to protect the elderly.

EXEMPT VS. NON-EXEMPT ASSET GIFTING

Imagine this: If Grandmother transfers $300,000 of stocks, bonds and cash to her heirs, she will be ineligible for Medi-Cal benefits for a long time.

Contrast that with the following scenario for transferring Grandmother's $300,000 residence. Grandmother moves into a Medi-Cal certified nursing home. She qualifies for benefits by bringing her non-exempt resources below $2,000. As part of her application, she declares on the Medi-Cal application her intent to return home. This action makes her home exempt for Medi-Cal qualifying and eligible to be transferred without affecting eligibility.

After qualifying for Medi-Cal long-term care benefits, Grandmother may transfer her $300,000 home to anyone. If she or her legal agent follows Medi-Cal's proscribed guidelines for transferring an exempt residence, she will not lose her eligibility. Additionally, this transfer may move her house out of her estate and likely out of reach of Medi-Cal Recovery officials.

NOTE: Gifting exempt and non-exempt resources involves financial and legal considerations that are outside the purview of this consumer-oriented publication. Just as medical journals inform consumers about complex medical procedures without recommending do-it-yourself surgery, this book alerts consumers to the breadth of gifting possibilities without recommending self-inflicted gifting disasters. For guidance on gifting issues, seek professional guidance.

GIFTING DISCOURAGED

Given that Medicaid/Medi-Cal is designed to help individuals and couples of limited financial means, Congressional authors of Medicaid legislation understandably frown upon people purposely reducing their assets through gifting strategies. Several times Congress has passed legislation either outlawing gifting by individuals who subsequently apply for benefits or outlawing professionals from advising individuals how to gift assets and later qualify for benefits. To date, this legislation has not been enforceable, yet these actions by members of Congress clearly indicate their attitudes towards this issue.

Of all volatile issues that families can fight about, certainly near the top of the list stands the subject of parents gifting assets to their children. "Wait until I'm dead before you come around looking for money" is the attitude of many seniors, while potential heirs question "Do you really want all of your hard-earned money to go to the government when you die?"

How will your family members handle these and other sensitive issues? The following chapter provides assistance to help families measure the strength of their family ties and identify hot-button issues.

CHAPTER 14

HOW STRONG ARE YOUR FAMILY TIES?

When you step forward, will your parents step back?

PEOPLE REMEMBER BETTER positive rather than negative family events and issues, according to a recent study. We want to believe good things about our respective families, so we smooth over the sharp edges of harsh words from bygone quarrels. With our parents, we tend to remember earlier days when they were not beset by persistent pain and discomfort. We minimize differences so we can feel better about them.

Unfortunately, when late-in-life crises arise, this tendency to minimize unresolved differences may lead to painful confrontations. For example, a daughter who has a strong need of parental approval may be irreparably hurt when either or both parents interpret her well-meaning inquiries about finances as underhanded maneuvers to get her inheritance early.

I have seen this happen among friends and clients. In one instance, a female client in her mid-40s was so taken back by her father's anger that she pulled back completely from involvement in their planning. "I just can't believe that he is acting this way," she confided sorrowfully.

His actions were not surprising to me. I had met her father several years earlier and felt firsthand the depth of his suspicions towards anyone who asked questions about his legal or financial affairs. I also witnessed his patronizing treatment towards his wife and her docile acceptance of his dominant manners. After that meeting I concluded that the father's domineering attitudes did not allow the family to work well together, a supposition that was confirmed later by his open distrust of the most loyal of his three daughters.

Witnessing firsthand these awful emotional collisions has led me to develop questionnaires to highlight the strengths and weaknesses of family emotional ties. I have labeled the numerical scores of these questionnaires as the Family Ties Quotient (FTQ).

These questionnaires, while not scientific, can indicate the strength of familial bonds among parents and their children. During my 14+ years of conducting family consultations, I have identified three loose classifications of family ties: great, mixed and terrible.

Great FTQ families come closest to the Leave-it-to-Beaver ideal of family relations. Dad and Mom know their life spans are limited. While each still has his and her full faculties they seek legal and financial assistance to set their affairs in order. They execute power of attorney documents for asset management and health care. They establish a trust and complete their burial arrangements. They conduct family meetings where their arrangements are discussed openly.

When Dad or Mom suffers a severe health setback, each family member knows how the legal and financial matters will unfold. This certainty better enables family members to support each other through the progressive stages of grieving.

In my unscientific sampling, approximately 20% of families enjoy such positive relations. Delightful clients, these families normally have strong spiritual centers.

At the opposite end of the FTQ spectrum reside fractured, dysfunctional families. These people make terrible clients. Fears of an uncertain afterlife cause parents to cling desperately to life. Either no legal and financial plans have been set in place and members flail about angrily, or legal and financial plans have been executed that pit family members against one another. Bitter lawsuits and hateful actions poison family relations for succeeding generations. From my experience, approximately 20% of families suffer such terrible relations.

That leaves 60% of families exhibiting mixed FTQ characteristics. Legal and financial plans may or may not exist. If they exist, such plans may be incomplete or outdated. Spiritual values range dramatically. Individual family members vary in knowledge about long-term care issues. Some family members feel validated, others feel betrayed. These families muddle through end-of-life crises, with many members mourning fitfully for years afterward.

These questionnaires were developed to help adult offspring identify positive and negative parental traits and devise action plans suited to their situation. My scoring reflects the 20-60-20 percentages discussed above.

Family Ties Quotient Scoring

Great:	168 to 134
Mixed:	134 to 34
Terrible:	34 to 28

I welcome input from psychologists, psychiatrists, grief counselors, priests, rabbis, ministers, spiritual counselors, social workers and other professional behaviorists regarding the strengths and weaknesses of the following questionnaires. I also welcome recommendations and criticisms from consumers. My goal is to incorporate your recommendations into future editions.

Measure your family ties quotient (FTQ) – Father version

My father respects my judgment on money and legal issues.

Strongly Agree	Mildly Agree	Agree	Disagree	Mildly Disagree	Strongly Disagree
6	5	4	3	2	1

My father respects my personal choices of friends and career.

Strongly Agree	Mildly Agree	Agree	Disagree	Mildly Disagree	Strongly Disagree
6	5	4	3	2	1

My father views death as the natural conclusion of the cycle of life.

Strongly Agree	Mildly Agree	Agree	Disagree	Mildly Disagree	Strongly Disagree
6	5	4	3	2	1

My father approves of my choice of marriage partner(s).

Strongly Agree	Mildly Agree	Agree	Disagree	Mildly Disagree	Strongly Disagree
6	5	4	3	2	1

My father approves of my methods of raising his grandchildren.

Strongly Agree	Mildly Agree	Agree	Disagree	Mildly Disagree	Strongly Disagree
6	5	4	3	2	1

My father treats my mother/his current wife courteously.

Strongly Agree	Mildly Agree	Agree	Disagree	Mildly Disagree	Strongly Disagree
6	5	4	3	2	1

My father tries to treat all of his children equally.

Strongly Agree	Mildly Agree	Agree	Disagree	Mildly Disagree	Strongly Disagree
6	5	4	3	2	1

My father attends important family gatherings.

Strongly Agree	Mildly Agree	Agree	Disagree	Mildly Disagree	Strongly Disagree
6	5	4	3	2	1

My father shares with at least one of his children his financial and legal arrangements.

Strongly Agree	Mildly Agree	Agree	Disagree	Mildly Disagree	Strongly Disagree
6	5	4	3	2	1

My father avoids contentious topics at family gatherings.

Strongly Agree	Mildly Agree	Agree	Disagree	Mildly Disagree	Strongly Disagree
6	5	4	3	2	1

My father is not bitter about his life choices.

Strongly Agree	Mildly Agree	Agree	Disagree	Mildly Disagree	Strongly Disagree
6	5	4	3	2	1

My father has social and personal support from established friends.

Strongly Agree	Mildly Agree	Agree	Disagree	Mildly Disagree	Strongly Disagree
6	5	4	3	2	1

My father wants to pass assets to his family.

Strongly Agree	Mildly Agree	Agree	Disagree	Mildly Disagree	Strongly Disagree
6	5	4	3	2	1

My father usually seeks professional legal and financial guidance on important matters.

Strongly Agree	Mildly Agree	Agree	Disagree	Mildly Disagree	Strongly Disagree
6	5	4	3	2	1

Total your score: ______

Now complete the next questionnaire.

Measure your family ties quotient (FTQ) – Mother version

My mother respects my judgment on money and legal issues.

Strongly Agree	Mildly Agree	Agree	Disagree	Mildly Disagree	Strongly Disagree
6	5	4	3	2	1

My mother respects my personal choices of friends and career.

Strongly Agree	Mildly Agree	Agree	Disagree	Mildly Disagree	Strongly Disagree
6	5	4	3	2	1

My mother views death as the natural conclusion of the cycle of life.

Strongly Agree	Mildly Agree	Agree	Disagree	Mildly Disagree	Strongly Disagree
6	5	4	3	2	1

My mother approves of my choice of marriage partner(s).

Strongly Agree	Mildly Agree	Agree	Disagree	Mildly Disagree	Strongly Disagree
6	5	4	3	2	1

My mother approves of my methods of raising her grandchildren.

Strongly Agree	Mildly Agree	Agree	Disagree	Mildly Disagree	Strongly Disagree
6	5	4	3	2	1

My mother treats my father/her current husband courteously.

Strongly Agree	Mildly Agree	Agree	Disagree	Mildly Disagree	Strongly Disagree
6	5	4	3	2	1

My mother tries to treat all of her children equally.

Strongly Agree	Mildly Agree	Agree	Disagree	Mildly Disagree	Strongly Disagree
6	5	4	3	2	1

My mother attends important family gatherings.

Strongly Agree	Mildly Agree	Agree	Disagree	Mildly Disagree	Strongly Disagree
6	5	4	3	2	1

My mother shares with at least one of her children her financial and legal arrangements.

Strongly Agree	Mildly Agree	Agree	Disagree	Mildly Disagree	Strongly Disagree
6	5	4	3	2	1

My mother avoids contentious topics at family gatherings.

Strongly Agree	Mildly Agree	Agree	Disagree	Mildly Disagree	Strongly Disagree
6	5	4	3	2	1

My mother is not bitter about her life choices.

Strongly Agree	Mildly Agree	Agree	Disagree	Mildly Disagree	Strongly Disagree
6	5	4	3	2	1

My mother has social and personal support from established friends.

Strongly Agree	Mildly Agree	Agree	Disagree	Mildly Disagree	Strongly Disagree
6	5	4	3	2	1

My mother wants to pass assets to her family.

Strongly Agree	Mildly Agree	Agree	Disagree	Mildly Disagree	Strongly Disagree
6	5	4	3	2	1

My mother usually seeks professional legal and financial guidance on important matters.

Strongly Agree	Mildly Agree	Agree	Disagree	Mildly Disagree	Strongly Disagree
6	5	4	3	2	1

Total your score for mother's questionnaire ________

Total your score for father's questionnaire ________

TOTAL ________

FAMILY TIES QUOTIENT SCORING

Great:	168 to 134
Mixed:	134 to 34
Terrible:	34 to 28

Completing the questionnaire for both of your parents may help you identify a decided difference of patterns between your parents. You may also understand better how their views shape your interactions with your immediate family. For further insight, you may ask your spouse or partner to complete these questionnaires about your parents.

Your goal is not to pass judgment on your parents or nurture old grudges and hurts. Your goal is to evaluate with clear vision the strength and weaknesses of your family ties so you can better assist your parents through their last years.

The task is not easy. As the natural cycle of life affects your family, you become the parent to your aging parents. You are still their child, yet you are expected to make adult decisions for them. Hopefully, measuring your family ties quotient will better help you navigate these challenging years with more understanding and less emotional turmoil in their house–and yours.

CHAPTER 15

CLOSING THOUGHTS

When Medi-Cal seems likely in your future

THROUGHOUT THIS BOOK we have discussed how to obtain Medi-Cal eligibility for seriously ill single or married individuals. We have also discussed planning for future long-term needs for younger individuals who can qualify financially and medically for long-term care insurance. However, we have not addressed the needs of individuals who do not qualify financially and/or medically for long-term care insurance and may need Medi-Cal assistance in the future.

If you or someone you know fit into this category, refer to the *Put it in a Box*™ worksheets on pages 125–126. Assets that fit into exempt boxes should be liquidated last when paying for an ill person's pre-nursing home care. This means that IRA assets should be spent last, not first. For similar reasons a person's residence should be the last asset to be liquidated to pay for care.

Exempt assets also provide seniors the greatest opportunity to win the trifecta of Medi-Cal planning: Control your assets during pre-nursing home care, exempt them to qualify for Medi-Cal nursing home benefits and pass them to your offspring out of reach of Medi-Cal Recovery.

Effective Medi-Cal planning is similar to effective tax or estate planning: Preparation pays. And in the same way smart consumers use qualified tax and estate planning experts to stay abreast of regulatory changes, individuals who see Medi-Cal in their respective futures should seek qualified assistance to plan effectively for an eventual Medi-Cal application.

Expect to see Medi-Cal eligibility rules tightened in the future. In the aftermath of the worst stock market declines since the Great Depression and a general decline of national wealth, taxpayers are pressuring elected officials at state and federal levels to curb government spending. Medicaid spending will likely be scrutinized, with special attention focused on benefits awarded to illegal immigrants and high net worth individuals. 'Medi-Cal for Millionaires' is certainly not the intention of these aid programs. Underlying the political debates will be the simple question: Who should qualify for taxpayer-funded government assistance?

Expect to see Medi-Cal eligibility rules tightened in the future

To keep consumers and advisors abreast of changes in Medi-Cal regulations and to promote informed discourse on long-term care issues, we will provide periodic relevant information on our website www.savingmomanddad.com.

Our website will also provide a forum for individuals to share personal solutions for care-giving challenges for others grappling with similar end-of-life issues.

My final discussion point arises from my observations of family interactions. As I explained in the section 'How strong are your family ties?' I observe that only twenty percent of families enjoy strong, positive family ties. Members of these admirable families care about each other and communicate that caring regularly. Nurtured by years of open communication and bolstered typically by strong spiritual beliefs, family members lovingly support their dying members through their passage out of this life and into the afterlife.

Those results come from a lifetime of sharing and support. As Samuel Butler in 1663 wisely observed:

As the ancients
Say wisely, have a care o' the' main chance,
And look before you ere you leap;
For as you sow, ye are like to reap.

We all want to arrive at our last days feeling loved, appreciated and cradled by the caring feelings of our families. To receive that positive support, we must nurture our close relationships with the same kind of love and appreciation we hope to receive.

To Anthea: Ah, My Anthea!

Give me a kiss, and to that kiss a score;
Then to that twenty, add a hundred more:
A thousand to that hundred: so kiss on,
To make that thousand up a million.
Treble that million, and when that is done,
Let's kiss afresh, as when we first begun.

—ROBERT HERRICK (1591-1674)

DETAIL, MISSOURI STONE BARN, FEBRUARY 2002

NICHOLS' ROUND BARN, NOVEMBER 2003

AFTERWORD

To the Virgins, to Make Much of Time
Gather ye rosebuds while ye may,
Old Time is still a-flying:
And this same flower that smiles today
Tomorrow will be dying.

—Robert Herrick (1591-1674)

EARLIER WE MET SUE and followed with her through her difficult days as she loved and cared for Howard, her husband.

For couples yet to face a health crisis, Sue offers these practical recommendations:

- See an attorney to complete a trust and power of attorney;
- Make sure you have flexibility in your estate planning documents to accommodate various scenarios.

If it becomes necessary to place your loved one in a nursing home, she recommends visiting the facility at differing times of day. "Go in (to the facility) anytime night or day. And if they won't let you in, move to another place," she states emphatically. Above all, visit regularly: "If you're not there, they don't get the care," she declares.

Sue is grateful that Medi-Cal regulations allowed her to keep all of their invested assets for her needs. Yet she wishes now they had spent more of their money having fun while Howard was still healthy.

Sue had to push her husband to spend money on travel. They flew to Hawaii only after their son enticed them with a $2,000 gift certificate. When they arrived, their son recommended they rent a convertible to drive around the islands. "Howard said 'No, that will cost more money,' but I said 'Let's do it!' " recounts Sue: "We had lots of fun, our son driving his convertible and we driving ours. I regret that I did not push Howard more often to spend money. Now I have the money but he's not here to enjoy it with me."

"Money is not everything," she advises: "Build memories together while you can."

SUSAN AND ELIZABETH, SISTERS

SHARE YOUR NURTURING KNOWLEDGE

We want to include contributions from our readers on www.savingmomanddad.com. Caring for aging family members requires many talents and we encourage experienced caregivers to share their tips for meeting daily challenges and problems.

Guidance for all areas is welcome. These may include tips for daily caregiving, working with legal and financial advisors, dealing with family relations: namely, anything that has helped you help your loved ones. We will identify you if you want recognition, or you may contribute anonymously. Your contributions may be mailed to Saving Mom and Dad Institute, 818 N Mountain Avenue, Suite 102, Upland, CA 91786. You may also submit contributions directly through our website.

We also want to print nostalgic, loving photographs sent by readers. You may include a loving tribute to a family member with your submitted photograph. Please send us a copy of your photograph. We can't assume responsibility for tracking and returning original photographs. Also, please understand that we must have permission from all living people pictured in a family photograph before we can print it.

We look forward to your loving contributions.

Basking in the Sunlight
Dave's cat 1974

GLOSSARY OF MEDI-CAL TERMS

After-acquired CSRA assets: Assets acquired by a Well Spouse after the month of application.

Community Spouse Resource Allowance (CSRA): The amount of non-exempt resources a Well Spouse may keep and qualify his/her spouse for Medi-Cal long-term care benefits. If the Well Spouse's income is low, this annual figure may be increased through a fair hearing or court petition.

Exempt assets: These are assets that an individual or married couple may own and qualify for Medi-Cal benefits. Included in this category are a residence, a vehicle, term life insurance, irrevocable burial arrangements, IRA and other tax-qualified accounts, and $2,000 of non-exempt assets.

Ill Spouse: Also known as the Institutionalized Spouse, this individual is the applicant for Medi-Cal benefits.

Medicaid/Medi-Cal: Health insurance program funded with federal money and administered through state and county governments to assist individuals who lack sufficient assets and/or income to pay for their medical care.

Medi-Cal certified facility: A health care facility that accepts Medi-Cal payments

Medicare: Federal program that provides health insurance coverage for people age 65 and older, and disabled individuals under age 65.

Minimum Monthly Maintenance Needs Allowance (MMMNA): If a Well Spouse does not have sufficient income in his/her name to meet the MMMNA, then Medi-Cal will allow allocation of income from the Ill Spouse to the Well Spouse to bring the Well Spouse's income up to the Minimum Monthly Maintenance Needs Allowance. Note: If a Well Spouse has income in excess of the MMMNA, this does not disqualify his/her spouse. Rather, this means the Well Spouse will keep all of his/her income and receive no allocation of income from the Ill Spouse's income.

Month of application: Medi-Cal handles applications on a month-by-month basis. If an applicant meets Medi-Cal qualifications on the last day of a month, then the applicant is eligible for the entire month.

Non-exempt assets: These are assets–also known as resources–that do not fit into an exempt category.

Notice of Action: Any time Medi-Cal makes a decision on an application, a Notice of Action is sent to the applicant. The backside of these notices contains phone numbers and instructions telling applicants how to appeal decisions.

Over property: Medi-Cal uses 'property' to describe any asset that can be turned to cash to pay for medical care. A finding of *over property* means the applicant had too many countable assets to qualify for a specific Medi-Cal program. 'Real property' refers to real estate. Usually a list of property values as calculated by Medi-Cal is included with a Notice of Action. When checking Medi-Cal's calculations, remember that income does not count as property in the month of receipt.

Recovery: A Medi-Cal program that recovers from the estates of deceased Medi-Cal recipient's money that was paid for the deceased individual's long-term care.

Redetermination: Every twelve months Medi-Cal requires that an individual's assets and income be re-evaluated to determine if he/she is still eligible to receive benefits.

Retroactive coverage: An applicant may apply for retroactive benefits for up to three months prior to the month of application. This is useful if the applicant can show that he/she is eligible for those months. Retroactive coverage often becomes available as part of an expansion of the Community Spouse Resource Allowance.

Share of cost: Commonly abbreviated to SOC, this describes the amount of money that an individual must pay to a long-term care facility out of his/her monthly income. Comparable to a co-payment for medical services.

Spend down: Describes process whereby an individual or married couple spends their money down to a level where they qualify for Medi-Cal benefits.

Supplemental Security Income (SSI): Supplemental income for people age 65 or older, or blind or disabled who have limited income and financial resources. Effective January 2004 the SSI payment for an eligible individual is

$564 per month and $846 per month for an eligible couple. Non-exempt resources may not exceed $2,000 for individuals, $3,000 for couples. SSI is part of the safety net for poor people. SSI recipients automatically qualify for Medi-Cal benefits.

Well Spouse: Also known as the At-home Spouse, this individual is allowed to keep certain levels of assets and income to maintain his/her standard of living.

Bob's Distant Relatives

$$ Put it in a Box™

ASSETS — Single Person

Residence	Vehicle	Term life insurance	Burial	IRA	Property Reserve

NON-EXEMPT RESOURCES

Bank accounts, CDs	$
Additional vehicles (Kelly Blue Book value)	
Cash value life insurance (cash surrender value)	
Rental real estate (assessed value, not FMV)	
Investment accounts (stocks, bonds, etc.)	
Other	
Total	$
Subtract $2,000 Property Reserve	(2,000) → Property Reserve
Excess non-exempt resources	$

INCOME

Social security	$
Pension	$
IRA Income	$
Total	$
Less maintenance need	$
Share of cost	$

$$ **Put it in a Box™**

ASSETS — Married Couple, one person in long-term care

Residence	Vehicle	Term life insurance	Burial	IRA	Property Reserve
					$2,000

Community Spouse Resource Allowance (CSRA)

NON-EXEMPT RESOURCES

Checking and savings accounts	$
Certificates of deposit (CDs)	$
Additional Vehicles	$
Cash value life insurance	$
Rental real estate (assessed value)	$
Investment accounts	$
Any other assests	$
Total	$
Property Reserve	$ (2,000)
CSRA (20___ limit)	$
Excess non-exempt resources	$

INCOME

	His	Hers
Social security	$_____	$_____
Pension	$_____	$_____
IRA Income	$_____	$_____
Investment income	$_____	$_____
Total	$_____	$_____
Maintenance Need	$_____	$_____
Allocation	$_____	$_____
Share of cost	$_____	$_____
Well spouse monthly income	$_____	$_____

Minimum Monthly Maintenance Needs Allowance (MMMNA)
20__ limit = $_____

NOTES

NOTES

www.savingmomanddad.com